The Journey of Women Leaders

Strength in Every Step

Helene Johnson,
Linda Cureton,
Jaclyn Rubino,
Tiffany Bailey

The Journey of Women Leaders

Copyright © 2025 by Helene Johnson, Linda Cureton, Jaclyn Rubino, and Tiffany Bailey. Printed in the United States of America. No part of this book may be used or reproduced in any manner whatsoever without written permission except for brief quotations embedded in critical articles and reviews. For information, email info@muse-technologies.com

Published by:

Muse

Muse Technologies, Inc.
4601 Presidents Drive
Suite 240
Lanham, MD 20706

Digital ISBN: 979-8-9929301-2-2

Trade Paperback ISBN: 979-8-9929301-1-5

Hardback ISBN 979-8-9929301-0-8

Contents

Introduction 1

Chapter 1: Who Am I? 5
    Helene 6
    Linda 13
    Jackie 18
    Tiffany 21

Chapter 2: The Misunderstood Woman 25
    Helene 26
    Linda 32
    Jackie 35
    Tiffany 41

Chapter 3: Poor Behavior —How Women Treat Women
.... 45
    Helene 46
    Linda 50
    Jackie 54
    Tiffany 58

Chapter 4: Big Girls Do Cry 63
    Helene 64
    Linda 67
    Jackie 70
    Tiffany 74

Chapter 5: Mansplaining 79
    Helene 80

Linda	83
Jackie	85
Tiffany	88

Chapter 6: Finding Balance 91

Helene	92
Linda	95
Jackie	98
Tiffany	104

Chapter 7: The Impostor Syndrome 109

Helene	110
Linda	115
Jackie	118
Tiffany	122

Chapter 8: Ageism 127

Helene	128
Linda	133
Jackie	135
Tiffany	140

Chapter 9: Your Seat at the Table 145

Helene	146
Linda	150
Jackie	153
Tiffany	158

Afterword 161

About the Authors 163

Introduction

Dear Sister,

We stare at our degrees, gilded trophies of a hard-fought education. They promised a clear path, a future paved with limitless potential, yet years into our careers, the landscape looks different. It's a terrain riddled with unexpected obstacles—the mansplaining colleague drowning out your voice in a meeting, the subtle undermining by other women vying for the same promotion. Ageism whispers that older workers are "overqualified" instead of "experienced." We've battled the suffocating grip of self-doubt, the societal pressure to be a flawless superwoman at home and a warrior in the boardroom, all while navigating a world that seems perpetually surprised by our ambition.

But through it all, there's been a constantly fierce determination to succeed, to carve our own space in a world that often tries to shrink us. This book is a testament to that fight. It's a collection of hard-won wisdom; a sisterly hand extended across the years to guide you and remind you that you are not alone on this journey.

These pages are filled with stories, both cautionary and triumphant. We'll delve into the subtle and overt biases women face, the importance of allyship, and the power of embracing your emotions—even the tears that some might misinterpret as weakness. We'll celebrate the unique strengths that come with age and experience and the importance of finding balance (whatever that may look like for you) in a world that demands your all.

Remember the Girl You Were?

Close your eyes for a moment and rewind. Recall the little girl you once were, bursting with unrestrained dreams. She wasn't afraid to climb the tallest tree, voice an opinion louder than anyone else's, or chase ambitions with unwavering belief. Somewhere along the way, society chipped away at that audacious spirit, whispering doubts and limitations. But that spark is still there, waiting to be rekindled.

This book is a call to reclaim that audacious spirit. It's a call to arms for the women who dream big, who refuse to be confined by expectations. It's a call to sisterhood, a reminder that we are stronger together, lifting each other as we rise.

Here, you'll find real-life stories—tales of victories hard-earned, setbacks overcome, moments when we stumbled and rose again, bruised but unbroken. We'll dissect the challenges we've faced, from the microaggressions that wear down our confidence to the blatant sexism that tries to silence us.

We'll discuss the importance of finding your voice and learning to speak with conviction and clarity, even when your voice trembles. We'll also unpack the complexities of navigating office politics, the delicate dance of forging alliances with women and men, and the art of building a support network that empowers you to reach your full potential.

Beyond the Workplace: Embracing Your Whole Self

This book isn't just about navigating the professional world. It's about nurturing the woman you are becoming in all aspects of your life. We'll delve into the ever-present struggle of balancing career aspirations, personal passions, and the desire to create a fulfilling life. We'll celebrate the strength it takes to say no, prioritize your well-being, and redefine success on your terms.

We'll also address the emotional complexities women often face in the workplace—the tears that well up during a frustrating meeting and the anger that simmers beneath the surface when faced with injustice. These are not signs of weakness but depth and resilience. We'll learn to embrace these emotions, to use them as fuel for transformation, and to challenge the societal narratives that try to silence us.

A Journey of Self-Discovery

This book is more than a collection of advice. It's a framework for self-discovery. We'll explore strategies for overcoming the impostor syndrome, that nagging voice that tells you you don't belong or haven't earned your accomplishments. We'll discuss the importance of mentorship and finding women who inspire you and can offer valuable guidance on your journey. Most importantly, we'll encourage you to embrace continuous learning, challenge yourself to step outside your comfort zone, and never stop growing.

As you turn the pages, sister, remember you are not on this path alone. We are here, a sisterhood forged in the fires of shared experiences, offering encouragement and support. Let's rewrite the script together, shattering glass ceilings, owning our power, and defining success on our terms. This is your story, your journey, your time to shine.

Chapter 1:
Who Am I?

Identity is the foundation of leadership, shaped by our personal histories, challenges, and triumphs. In this chapter, we share the unique journeys that define our sense of self. Through stories of resilience, transformation, and ambition, we explore how our identities influence our leadership styles and career paths. Reflect on your own journey as you discover the power of embracing who you are.

Helene

My name is Helene Johnson. I am a mother of three wonderful daughters, a grandmother (Bubbie) of amazing grandchildren, a wife of a sweet man, a sister, an aunt, and a cousin. My father was a Holocaust survivor, and my mother was an artist and stay-at-home mom.

Career-wise, for forty-five years, I have worked in some form or another in the information technology (IT) field. I've worked in the government industry for the last twenty years, focusing on strategy, business development, and technology. I came to this field because my parents were convinced that I would starve if I were to do what I wanted to do, which was to teach elementary school. In my junior year at the University of Maryland, they told me I had to move home, transfer to the University of Baltimore, and study computer sciences. I had no idea what a computer was then, but I did as they wished and committed to my new school. I had one year to learn all about computers. I even got a job working in the data center. I was all in!

A year after I transferred, I graduated and entered the work world.

My first job was as an IT intern at Miami Dade County in Miami, Florida. It was time to move out of Maryland. I loved my job! I met many great people and was a blank slate, ready to absorb everything people would teach me. I found out that not only did I like computer programming, but I was pretty good at it. I took on more and more tasks and excelled, but I missed my family and friends and hated the bugs and critters in Miami. So, after a few years, my brother got me a job at Westinghouse in Maryland. I packed up my bags and moved back to Baltimore.

Five years after graduation, I got married and eventually had three daughters. I loved (still do) being a mom, but I was already torn. I wanted to be a "traditional mom" who was available for all school events and was home in the afternoon when the kids came home from school. However, I also wanted a career, and part-time was unacceptable in my field back then. I loved what I did for a living—the paycheck and learning. I moved into management roles and continued excelling, but I was conflicted! The guilt was overwhelming. Despite that, my husband and I made it work, and our daughters thrived.

My first job in the federal IT community came when Lockheed Martin hired me to support the Social Security Administration as a task order manager focused on the application side of the agency. In five years, I went from a task order manager to an area lead and then to a deputy program manager supporting the Environmental Protection Agency.

My next big break came when a recruiter approached me to apply for the position of Deputy Chief Information Officer for the Department of Education, Student Financial Aid. This was a massive leap for me. Not only would I be an executive in the federal government, but I would also be wearing the hat of a customer to industry. With Lockheed Martin, I was a contractor supporting the government. Now, I was about to be in the government. What a fantastic opportunity! I knew this was a game-changer.

I learned so much at this job. I traveled nationwide and spoke in front of huge audiences. I was the head of the agency's application development group. As a federal employee, I received my Master of Science in organizational transformation from Johns Hopkins, and my thesis focused on trust between industry and government. It was timely and valuable as I navigated being on the "other side."

I left the government after two years when I was forty years old. I was more comfortable providing support and services to the government than depending on contractors to support me while in the government. My next twelve years were spent moving from company to company, picking up new skills and areas of responsibility. I went from program leadership to business development. I found that I loved building relationships and selling to the government. I had understood the government buyer role since I was one earlier in my career.

I loved my career but did not love missing so much time with my family. I was focused on becoming successful, and this came at a cost. I would have balanced that more if I could have done anything differently. But we had money to give our daughters an excellent education, be involved in many activities, and have a great childhood. I have regrets, but I have learned that it does not help to look backward in your life. You must adjust, learn, and keep pushing forward.

My husband and I divorced during this period, and I remarried. This decision impacted my family and added to my guilt, but sometimes, one must make the best decisions for happiness and well-being. Fortunately, I am still good friends with my ex-husband. I am so thankful for his friendship.

I was more than thirty years into my career and in my early fifties. I was also going through treatment for breast cancer, which set me back physically, emotionally, and professionally. I needed time to recover and clear my brain fog. Because of the treatment, I believed I was not as sharp as I used to be, which was evident to my employer. I can tell you that being a worker in your early fifties is not for the timid. I was no longer seen as a high-potential person. I made more money than my younger peers. By my mid-fifties, it seemed like every time I was hired by a new company, before long, I was asked to document my job and mentor people younger than me. Then, when I shared everything that I knew, I realized I was no longer needed. I'm the first to admit that I was hurt by how my career took a hit. I was on the rise, and then boom, I was done. Or so I thought.

I met a man who was a career mentor/coach. He was not formally trained in this field. He relied on his life experience. He had templates and tools, which were helpful. But what he did for me was teach me how to create the me I wanted to be. He showed me that it was not a company that could bring down my career. He taught me I wasn't a middle-aged woman who made a high salary and could be replaced by someone younger. He cared about me, believed in me, and helped me believe in myself. He also showed me at our first meeting that I was experiencing this phenomenon of hiring me, having me teach my replacement, and then shooing me out because I served my purpose. I was hired to solve a need and train others, and my time was temporary. He told me that I was being treated like a consultant. So, with his help and guidance, I realized I should be a consultant. That's when I decided to bite the bullet, build my own company, and make a go of it. My husband and I built and sold a nonprofit association focused on business development professionals. So, I built a for-profit company. My husband was gainfully employed, so I had some time to put the infrastructure in place and find clients. I named the company Bid2Win Consulting, and it took off. I had all the freedom I needed. I had a blog and a podcast. I was interviewed, I wrote articles, and I had a niche. I capitalized on my knowledge and successes. I was back, more robust and better than ever!

Before I knew it, I was sixty years old and started considering retiring. My husband, who was past retirement age, wanted to return to his childhood home state of Florida. It was his dream, and I wanted to ensure he would be happy and healthy in his retirement. So, we sold Bid2Win to a software company in 2021. I joined this company as their chief value officer. I brought to them my relationships and artifacts, as well as my expertise in strategy and business development. I was excited to see my processes embedded into a software program and the possibilities this brought to my field. And best of all, I could support them from Florida!

So, we packed up and moved. I love my home in Florida and how happy my husband is now. My only regret is that my daughters and their families are not here. They are all up north. I was missing out on living near my family and again conflicted. I always wanted to be a grandmother, and here I am, two-and-a-half hours of a plane ride away. So, we fixed that. We bought a home near family, and now, we are "snowbirds," splitting our time between Florida and Virginia. I wanted to have the best of both worlds. And when I am in Florida, I visit family as often as possible and thank goodness for technology (FaceTime, Facebook, and Instagram).

I am now sixty-five and not ready to retire. So, what's next? As I learned from my coach, no one except me will decide my plan. I am a doctorate in business administration candidate at the University of South Florida. I will graduate in 2026 and am the oldest in my class. Many people ask me why I have returned to school. Several have pointed out that they think I'm too old for this. One of my family members asked me, "Why are you doing this so late in life?"

I'm doing this for myself! It's on my bucket list, and I know I can do it. I look forward to the day my whole family celebrates with me when I receive my diploma.

I am still actively working as a strategic consultant, specializing in helping companies manage and optimize their intergenerational workforce. Through my company, **Next Wave Workforce Consulting**, I guide organizations in effectively engaging and supporting employees of all ages, ensuring they navigate workforce transitions—whether due to job loss, AI-driven changes, or an aging workforce—with care and strategy. By adopting this approach, companies can manage change responsibly while retaining and leveraging the invaluable knowledge of their workforce.

Having experienced my own career disruptions in my mid-fifties, I understand firsthand the importance of guidance and support during times of transition. Just as I once needed someone to help me regain control of my career, I now dedicate myself to doing the same for others, empowering them to adapt, thrive, and take charge of their professional futures.

I am also a co-writer of this book. I invited my three friends, Linda, Jackie, and Tiffany, to join me. We want to help other women navigate the ups and downs of being a professional woman, a mom, a wife, a caretaker, and a grandma, if that is in the future, along with the other roles we play. I want to help other women learn from my successes and the lessons learned. I want to use all my bumps in the road and show that I am proud of what I've accomplished and am living a great life. I am also a frequent flier up north to see my family, and I love being a Bubbie (grandmother). I also play golf and mah-jongg. And my husband and I are very happy Floridians and Virginians. So, as you can see, I am still a work in progress and will most likely be until my last breath.

Linda

My beginnings started in Washington, D.C., in a quaint area called Deanwood in the far northeast section of the city. This area was once farmland and eventually was home to some of the city's most prosperous African-American residents. The streets were lined with mulberry and weeping willow trees. We lived in my grandmother's house, a framed house built in 1914 that boasted a cherry tree and a grapevine with sour grapes. I went to D.C. public schools, graduating from the first class of the Duke Ellington School of the Arts in Northwest Washington, D.C., majoring in instrumental music. I graduated from Howard University with a mathematics major and a Latin minor. My graduate education continued in mathematics and finally with a Ph.D. in organizational leadership. I am currently the chief executive officer of a small business, Muse Technologies, Inc., which primarily provides management consulting and staffing services for the federal government.

How did I get from mulberries to Muse? The best answer I can offer is I don't know. Well, perhaps I do know. When I graduated from Charles Richard Drew Elementary School, I wanted to be a meteorologist—or was it my love of lying in a bed of clover looking up, watching the clouds go by as the branches of the weeping willow tree seemed to wave with approval? When I went to Kelly Miller Junior High School, I developed a tremendous crush on my algebra teacher, so it would make sense that I wanted to be a math teacher. Our family moved to a better neighborhood in Northwest Washington, D.C. where I joined the band even though I didn't play anything but the piano. But I was able to take that musical foundation and play most instruments. I settled on the French horn because my very best friend played the horn. I ended up at Duke Ellington following my BFF (best friend forever) Donna.

I didn't think about college until I got to the eleventh grade. I recall overhearing my mother talking to someone about me, saying she knew I wanted to go to college, but we had no means. For this reason, my mother took a job at Howard University, where we could take advantage of tuition remission. I heard no more talk about my college future than that phone call I overheard. I goofed around the house one September day, knowing I would return to school the following week. I remember it was the Wednesday before Labor Day. I would have been starting my twelfth-grade year the following week. I got a phone call telling me I was accepted into the High School College Internship Program (HISCIP). I had to report to Howard University the next day to register for my first year of college. Whew, child! It was a whirlwind day I was not prepared for. After registration, my fellow interns met with the dean. He asked us individually what we would major in, and everyone said pre-med. So, what would a seventeen-year-old first-year college student say? I said pre-med.

When I entered my sophomore year, my Latin teacher asked me about my major. He told me that every outstanding scholar must be something other than a pre-med major. He asked me what I love. I told him about mathematics and Latin. He assured me I would succeed if I majored in subjects I loved. In other words, passion—love for what you study—is necessary and *sufficient* for success. After that conversation, I marched into the counselor's office and changed my major to mathematics and my minor to Latin.

I enjoyed Latin, classical mythology, and mathematics. I was the typical dreamy mathematician-philosopher who enjoyed useless trivia and deductive reasoning. I pondered taking ancient Greek in my senior year but ran into a speed bump, which seemed like a roadblock at the time. My counselor said I had to take a computer course before graduating. I had no desire to comply. Thus, as any decent nineteen-year-old would do, I procrastinated until all the classes were filled. However, my resourceful counselor found a class in IBM Assembler Language that only had one student. The counselor registered me on the spot. I liked it, and it was not too unlike ancient Greek. After that, I took a FORTRAN class and graduated with honors. My next stop was graduate school, where I received a full scholarship to work on my master's and Ph.D. in mathematics. Then, *screech!* I met and got engaged to a cheap guy (yes, we eventually divorced). He wanted me to get a job so I could pay for a new master cylinder for my beloved Dodge Dart 225 Slant-Six. Reluctantly, I looked for a job. I was a procrastinating teenager, so I sauntered into the university's career day. The event was in a hot, stinky gymnasium. It was crowded, but I landed in the middle of a long line of potential employers spread alphabetically. I stood in front of the "Ns"—National Aeronautics and Space Administration (NASA) and the Nuclear Regulatory Commission (NRC). NASA seemed cool. Besides, I always wanted to be an astronaut but didn't see anyone who looked like me—a nearsighted, slightly overweight, Black female—then. I was interviewed by the notable Black inventor Valerie Thomas. NASA was looking for outstanding scholars who knew IBM Assembler and

FORTRAN. I gave up my dream of opining about differential equations and the Fourier series and started working for NASA as a GS-7 mathematician.

I had a seasonal job with the National Oceanic and Atmospheric Administration (NOAA) as a GS-2 student assistant cartographer. Cartographers (map makers) of that era used pen and ink to create nautical charts. But here's the problem: I am left-handed and kept smearing wet ink with my left hand. My supervisors were tired of fixing charts I ruined, so they sent me to work on the computers since no one else was interested.

Notably, my supervisors at NOAA and the counselor at Howard University imposed working on computers as a punishment. The irony is that I spent thirty-nine years in the U.S. federal government information technology (IT) field, rising to the rank of a cabinet-level chief information officer (CIO) in the prestigious senior executive service. Furthermore, I retired from NASA and founded an IT company that provides strategic IT services and staff augmentation.

So, who am I? I am not my occupation nor my academic major. I am not my accomplishments, nor am I my failures. Am I that little girl lying in the grass in the shade of a weeping willow tree, watching the clouds go by?

As I sit here now, reflecting on my journey from the mulberry tree–lined streets of Deanwood to founding Muse Technologies, I am filled with a deep sense of gratitude and wonder. My path has been anything but linear, filled with unexpected turns and serendipitous encounters. From dreaming under the weeping willow trees to navigating the hallowed corridors of Howard University, from the crowded gymnasium where I found NASA to the esteemed halls of the federal government, each experience has shaped who I am today.

But beyond the titles and the accolades, the true essence of my journey lies in the love and passion I discovered along the way. It's in the excitement of solving complex mathematical problems, the joy of exploring ancient languages, and the satisfaction of overcoming obstacles, whether academic challenges or the smudged ink of a left-handed cartographer. It's in the friendships forged, the mentors who guided me, and the resilience that grew from every setback.

So, who am I? I am a culmination of all these moments, both the planned and the unforeseen. I am the product of a community that believed in me, a family that supported me, and a personal drive that pushed me to explore the unknown. I am the little girl who found wonder in the world around her and carried that sense of curiosity and awe into every stage of her life.

I am a storyteller, weaving together the threads of my past with my future ambitions. Each chapter, from the mulberries of my childhood to the muse that inspires my work today, is a testament to the power of dreams and the relentless pursuit of one's passions. As I look ahead, I am excited to see where the next chapter will lead, knowing that the journey is as important as the destination. And through it all, I will continue to find joy in the simple, timeless act of laying in the grass, watching the clouds go by, and dreaming of what comes next.

Jackie

Hi! Let's take this opportunity for you to get to know me since we'll be together for nine chapters. I'm Jackie, more formally Jaclyn Smyth Rubino. I'm in my early forties, still working on navigating life and living it to its fullest potential. I'm married to my wonderful husband, Eric, and we live in Alexandria, Virginia. I'm proud of my Rhode Island roots and am an ocean girl at heart, although the mountains and ski slopes call my name, too.

I am currently a government executive with more than twenty years of work experience. How did I get here? Honestly, I thought corporate law would be my path in life. From the time I was a little girl, I desired to be an attorney. Not just any type of attorney, but a corporate lawyer. In undergraduate school in Rhode Island, I double majored in political science and business management. I had an opportunity to come to Washington, D.C., for a semester in my junior year to pursue an internship. What internship did I land? A coveted White House one, of course!

While in D.C., I fell in love—not with a man, but with the city. I loved its vibrancy; the people were interesting, self-motivated, and professional. I couldn't get enough. So, I made my way back to Rhode Island to finish college so I could return for good to the city I loved.

Within a few days of graduation in May 2004, I drove alone to D.C. to stay in a hotel, find a job, and secure housing for me and a college friend. I took my first job, an administrative assistant position at The Onyx Group, an architecture engineering firm in Alexandria, put a deposit on a townhouse to rent, and rushed home to officially pack for good.

After a short time as an administrative assistant in a small and growing firm, I was given additional duties in human resources (HR) since no one had encumbered such a position. I embraced the role and learned quite a bit about all things HR. Eventually, I moved to Smithsonian Business Ventures, where I continued my HR career. At this point, I recognized that I wanted to pursue a master's in business administration degree, so I started an accelerated program at George Washington University. By the time graduation was upon me, I had the opportunity to jump into the world of government consulting. After a few years of consulting, I became a government employee as I was seeking a work/life balance that was absent in my life (more on that later). I've been with the government since 2010.

I started my government career as a program analyst, and over time, demonstrated my capabilities and drove my path up the ladder to where I am today: a government executive. My path and experiences haven't always been easy. Finding myself as a leader has been quite an evolution and journey. But it has been one heck of a ride so far and something I'm excited to share with you.

So why are we here? The woman and leader I am today is not who I will be tomorrow or in the years to come. And she certainly isn't who she was twenty years ago! That same truth applies to you, too! What I've learned along the way: None of us are perfect, and we all have flaws. It is about the roadblocks you encounter in your journey and career that mold you. How you grow or bounce back from all that life throws your way molds you into the woman and leader you will be tomorrow. Opportunities to learn, grow, and evolve are constantly there—these chapters cover some of my evolution.

These pages follow stories about my life and career that have taught me valuable lessons. This book reflects what lessons I would want the blissfully ignorant twenty-something-year-old me with rose-colored glasses on to know that I wish I'd known then. I hope you learn something new that applies to your life and leadership journey as a woman. It's a shame that we have endured some of the topics in the chapters of this book as women. But the reality is that these topics bind us like a sisterhood, and so I hope you find some sense of solace knowing that you won't be the first or the last woman to endure these. So, when faced with these situations, I hope you can apply some of the advice I and my colleagues shared. Or, at the very least, think of it and know you are not alone.

Always remember to stay true to yourself and who you are authentically, but work to fine-tune and improve the version of *you* over time. Understand the truth that absolutely no one owes you anything. It's up to you to have the drive to make things happen, as doors don't open themselves! Give yourself some grace along the way in all aspects of your life. We're all human, we have flaws, and we make mistakes. How you learn, grow, and recover from those situations matters most.

Tiffany

My name is Tiffany, and my story begins in Gary, Indiana, a place known for its grit and resilience. Born to a teenage mother and raised in a city famous for Michael Jackson, steel mills, and a formidable reputation, I used to shy away from sharing where I was from. But now, I embrace it because Gary shaped me. It's a city that taught me the meaning of perseverance, and I carry that with me every day.

As an African American woman in my mid-40s, I stand at the intersection of many identities—daughter, mother, wife, executive, and author. My journey has been one of breaking barriers and defying expectations. I'm a mom to a beautiful daughter, a rising junior at Virginia Commonwealth University, and the wife of a wonderful husband who has stood by me through every challenge and triumph.

Professionally, I am the executive vice president of a mid-sized information technology firm in Bethesda, Maryland. My portfolio is a testament to my vision and commitment, earning accolades such as the prestigious Governor's Award for my work with small businesses. I am also a two-time best-selling author, driven by a passion to share my story and uplift others.

How did I get here?

My journey started long before titles and accolades—back at Vohr Elementary School, where I was just a little girl trying to find her way. I didn't have the head start many others had, but I had something even more powerful: the determination to succeed. My teachers pushed me, my grandmother disciplined me with love, and I learned early on that giving up was not an option.

As the eldest of six, I naturally assumed a leadership role at home and school. But while boys were praised for their leadership, I was labeled "bossy." Navigating the double standards of being a Black woman has been a lifelong challenge, but it has also been a source of my strength.

We lived paycheck to paycheck, but I knew education was my ticket out. I earned a full scholarship to the University of North Florida, where I balanced work and studies, determined to create a better future for myself.

My career began humbly in a call center, but I rose quickly with hard work and persistence. Promotions came, and soon, I was asked to relocate to Maryland to help expand operations—a move that would change my life. I took a leap of faith, and despite the challenges of being a young, ambitious mom in a new city, I thrived.

Years later, a recruiter's call introduced me to the Federal Deposit Insurance Corporation, a name unfamiliar to me then but one that would define a pivotal chapter in my career. I embraced the opportunity and agreed to an interview. I'll never forget the drive, over an hour to an office surrounded by towering glass windows. After meeting with the executive team, I sat in a conference room, waiting for the recruiter to walk me out. As I gazed out the window, I felt it, the weight of every struggle and sacrifice culminating in this very moment.

Everything I've done has been to make my grandmother proud. She was a woman who spent her life giving back to her community. In 2021, I launched the Joyce Anita Kikalos Foundation in her honor, providing scholarships to aspiring nurses—those who, like me, might not have all the advantages but have the drive to succeed.

What's next?

I'm not entirely sure, but the path forward is bright. Starting my own company is on the horizon—chief executive officer, that's a title I can get used to. But beyond titles, my mission is to continue empowering others, especially women who, like me, have had to reinvent themselves repeatedly to prove their worth.

I was honored to be invited to this project by my older sisters and co-writers, women I deeply respect and admire. I'm opening up like never before in the chapters ahead, sharing the lessons I've learned in more than forty years. This story is about resilience, reinvention, and the relentless pursuit of excellence. It's about finding strength in vulnerability, embracing your truth, and never being afraid to start over.

So, as you read on, know this: You are capable, you are worthy, and you belong—no matter where you come from or what the world says about you.

Chapter 2:
The Misunderstood Woman

Society often misinterprets women's strength and assertiveness as aggression or abrasiveness. In this chapter, we examine the stereotypes we face, from being labeled "bossy" to battling the "angry" trope. Through our honest experiences, we reveal the struggles of navigating these misconceptions while staying true to ourselves. Let's challenge these labels together and redefine what it means to lead with authenticity and boldness.

Helene

I have never been a cheerleader. I do remember wanting to be one as a young girl. I used to march down the sidewalk in front of my house, chanting cheers. My favorite one was popular at all the boys' sports games, and I used to love it. It was *"Be Aggressive. B.E. Aggressive, B.E.A.G.G.R.E.S.S.I.V.E."* It was a catchy tune with lots of stomping and clapping, with a lively message. It meant winning the game at any cost. Just beat them. The cheer I never heard, ever, was *"Be a bitch, B.E. a bitch."* I think it was because *bitch* is not the nicest word, but more likely because being a bitch will not help you get ahead, not as a team player or a leader. It doesn't help in any aspect of your life, whether being a parent, sibling, spouse, friend, coworker, or leader. Now, how about aggressiveness? Does that work in any of these roles? I think so but dialing it back to assertiveness and confidence may be best.

In my forties, as a deputy chief information officer (DCIO), one of the memories that defined my personality as a leader was fear. I knew the area for which I was responsible—software development. After all, I could code. I was good at that. But I was not hired to code. I was hired to ensure the agency had good code and processes to test and implement well. Instead of developing good software independently, I had to depend on others—contractors to write the code and my team to test and implement it. I had to lead this group and rely on others. I did this successfully but with an iron fist.

I still remember to this day what I used to tell my direct reports: *"I don't care how you do it, just don't drop a ball!"* That's right, I used to overcome my lack of control and ability to do what I knew needed to be done by scaring others into not messing up. If only I knew then what I know now: Putting fear into others to ensure you succeed is being a bitch. I did not care how it made them feel. I only cared about succeeding and looking good to the chief information officer.

Turns out, when I said what I thought, I was labeled as a bitch and aggressive. I never really understood why girls and women were uncomfortable with me until one day when my daughters were little, I went through their toy cabinet where they shoved everything—stray crayons, half-completed pictures, dried-up Play-Doh, and every doll and their clothes. The cabinet was packed, and I was trying to clear it out for the fifty millionth time. I was throwing things out onto the floor and just ranting. I was yelling at them, telling them how ridiculous it was to shove so much into this cabinet, and informing them that we would not buy them new school supplies because everything they needed was in there, just tossed in without any rhyme or reason. I saw their tears but was too engrossed in teaching them a lesson. Then, one of my daughters looked at me with so much sadness and said, "You are so mean that even my friends are scared of you!" I stopped dead in my tracks and just looked at the three most influential people in the world my daughters. Six blue eyes, all filled with tears. All caused by me.

Before you, the reader, wonder how I could have been so cruel, let me explain why I behaved like that. I did so because I knew this would cost extra money we did not need to spend. Could I justify spending money on more toys and school supplies when we had everything they needed in their toy cabinet? No matter who I hurt, I just said what I thought when I thought it. And if someone stood up to me as my daughter did, I fell apart—folded instantly. Even then, I had thin skin, and although I could dish it out, I could not take it.

My say-what-I-thought behavior continued throughout my career. I was always blunt. I honestly believed people would respect me more if I said things right to their face, not behind their back. But it backfired time and time again. I genuinely believe people were afraid of making me angry. I was told more times than I can remember that I had no filter. I just said what I thought, no matter the consequences. I realized this was very poor behavior until I had my own business thirty-five-plus years into my career. Yes, people knew that I was smart. They knew I was good at what I did. They knew that if they supported my vision, they could succeed. But they also learned to be careful around me. You would think that as I got older, I got nicer. I have, I believe, but it did not happen overnight. As a leader in companies and even in my personal life, I dialed back the bitchiness, but it took time. I still said what I thought needed to be done by others. I needed to convey what was required and trust my team to get it done.

Five years after the ball-dropping mantra, my company sent me to "charm school." This was a professional course where they made you self-aware through tests and role-playing. Based on my peers' tests and feedback in this course, I received a report, which identified what I was good at and what I could do better. I found out that I was good at understanding the big picture. I could easily articulate that I wanted a picture of a house, birds, grass, and trees. I even wanted a fireplace that only turned on when it was cold. I could quickly sketch out what I wanted, but I needed to figure out how to make this look good, drawn with dimension and color with a fireplace that only worked when it was cold. In other words, I was great at the big picture but should never take a role where I must be detail oriented.

That is when my career changed forever. I was a program manager for a large defense contractor during this course. I was the leader of a program supporting a federal agency. I had a staff of more than one hundred people, with lots of direct reports. Once again, it was focused on software development for the agency. I was hiring, motivating, training, empowering, and failing. Yes, I was a great leader (I thought); we were growing and doing well. But it was not me. It was my team. The competent people on my team were great at doing their jobs. I, on the other hand, was feeling nervous all the time. I had to ensure the train ran smoothly down the track while ensuring the riders (government customers) were happy and enjoying their ride. I also had to ensure that my direct reports were kept from showing me up so they could take my job. In other words, I had a job where I knew the big picture. I surrounded myself with people who could execute the plan, and they could not do that without me (again, so I thought). So, I had to stay relevant and confident, so everyone saw they needed my leadership. Too bad I turned out not to be so relevant.

Fast forward six months. I was given an experienced program manager as my deputy. In no time, I could see that she wanted my job, and she got it. It took her less than three months to show my management and the customer that she had a level of competency above mine. Boy was she aggressive! I had yet to learn how to handle this. I remember when my boss told me they would remove me and give her my role. I was angry and crushed. But mostly, I was relieved because I was exhausted. I was so tired of watching her go after my job. I was tired of putting myself down because I started to believe she was better than me. I was also tired of resenting her. And most of all, I was tired of being a program manager. As I learned in my charm course, I wanted to design more pictures without worrying about the execution.

The same boss who removed me from my program management position gave me a gift. He transferred me to a group that focused on growing the company from a business development perspective. In this new group, I was taught how to win new programs. The person leading the strategy to bid on new work is a capture manager. I had yet to learn what a capture manager did or if I could do the job, but the good news is that they were willing to teach me. It took me the better part of a year of on-the-job training, including shadowing experienced capture managers. Turns out I loved it and was good at it. The capture manager leads a team of people with different skills needed to develop a winning proposal. I had to lead people only in the short term—up to proposal time. And most of the teamwork is in the late stages of the capture. I could do most of the work myself and only call in folks when I needed their expertise. In other words, I had to ensure people knew the end goal, but I could do most things myself, leveraging the experts when needed. And I just needed to keep my management confident that I knew how to win. In other words, I had to exude confidence, lead the team, win the work, and then go off to win the next job with either the same experts or new ones if new skills and strategies were needed.

And that is how I lost the bitchiness and the aggressiveness and gained the confidence and maturity to *Be Assertive, B.E. Assertive!*

Now, I will share what I learned with you. I learned the importance of listening to lead. I realized that to succeed as a leader, you need to surround yourself with more intelligent and competent people than you. In other words, you do not have to do what you want done. You must have confidence in your team that they understand what needs to be done and will get it done. In a sporting team analysis, the coach is not out there playing. But if she has a great team with the right talent, and they know and execute the strategy, only then can they win. The coach must show confidence in her team and understand each player's strengths and attributes to enable them to play as a team. You must have the confidence to lead. From a leadership perspective, you must know your stuff and ensure your team knows the same stuff but much more profoundly than you. Determine what you are good at. What gets you going? What challenges you? And determine what you could be better at (for me, it is anything detail-oriented, along with leading a program). You will only have some of these answers right away. It took me fifteen years to figure that out, starting with charm school. Oh, and don't worry if you fail. Learn from that failure and adjust the course. Be assertive. Be confident. And remember, surround yourself with people more intelligent than you, and leverage them to hit your goals (in my case, to win the deal).

Most importantly, if anyone calls you a bitch to your face or behind your back, before you are one to them, try to understand what makes them think you are one. You will learn from it. You can adjust. You do not need to be nasty to get ahead and to fight off others. It would help if you were confident and willing to change yourself to be the most confident, successful leader in your field. So, why not wear those cheerleading shoes and stomp out a catchy tune?

Linda

In the musical *My Fair Lady*, Professor Henry Higgins asks the rhetorical question in the song "A Hymn to Him": Why can't a woman be more like a man? He thinks women are irrational, exasperating, irritating, vacillating, calculating, maddening, and infuriating. I will share two examples of where I was misunderstood.

Being *One of Those*. I was having happy hour with two of my African-American male colleagues. While talking, one of them asked me what university I attended. I answered Johns Hopkins. He looked at me, waiting for another answer. Then I said Howard University.

He said to me, "Figures!"

I said something to the effect of, what are you talking about (there may have been a profanity here or there)?

He said, "See? This is right here." It was a joke, all in fun, but something about me is very *Howard University*, whatever that is.

Howard University is a prestigious historically black university located in Washington, D.C. Howard University is committed to social justice and promoting civil rights and equality. The school boasts an influential alumni network and prepares its students for leadership roles. I was irritated that a Black, successful female executive was perceived as a bitch by supportive colleagues. But when my friend said, "Figures," maybe he saw a woman who had a voice and was not afraid to use it. Perhaps he saw a woman who had grit and resilience. Maybe I am more understood than it would appear.

Being Mad. The second example is with a boss that I had. I adored him, and we had a great relationship. But I'm not going to lie; I applied for the job he got. I should have gotten it, and it went to him. When he started the job, I still had a lot of anger about getting passed over (again). However, his personality and leadership skills softened my hardened heart. Eventually, I left the organization for a long-awaited promotion. At my going away party, he gave me a DVD gift. The DVD was *Diary of a Mad Black Woman*. I was not amused then.

I had to admit it to myself now that it was funny. His wife cautioned him about giving me the DVD. But, in retrospect, I was not a mad Black woman. I was mad. And I am a Black woman who was mad. Period.

Being Smart. I think well on my feet, have a good memory, and am a critical thinker. How could that be misunderstood? Well, yes, it can. I was making a presentation on a significant change in how our desktops would be deployed and supported. I understood the technology, the deployment strategy, and the risks. I ensured the risks were mitigated and contingency plans were in place. During the presentation, I was riddled with questions. The final question was, "You have an answer for everything, don't you?" I paused for several beats and looked thoughtfully in the air before I said yes (I think I may have been a wee bit sassy).

At this point in my life, I do not apologize for being a Black woman educated at Howard University. I recognize the bias associated with the mad Black woman. I also remember the bias related to the bias of "Oh, you're one of those *educated* ones" from Howard University.

I am who I am—a proud, educated Black woman. When dealing with people professionally and personally, I must know how I am being received and how stereotypes affect interactions. Nevertheless, I do not apologize, and neither should you.

In response to Professor Higgins, the question should not be why a woman cannot be more like a man but rather why we can't see and value each other as unique, competent, and resilient in our ways. We develop as individuals and a society through knowledge and acceptance of these variations. Of course, there were times in my career when I had to bite my tongue, play dumb, and smile through tears of anger. Today, I keep my head high, honestly reflecting on the qualities and values that have brought me thus far.

Jackie

Many of us are guilty of assigning labels to individuals or populations based on our unconscious biases, beliefs, and, quite typically, our narrow-minded observations. From a professional woman's perspective, one label that can hurt is the label of *bitch*. This term is used, in most instances, as an insulting way to describe a woman; very seldom do men suffer from such a label. According to *Merriam-Webster* dictionary online (because, let's face it, who has a hard copy dictionary anymore?), *bitch* as defined in the informal and often offensive meaning, is "a malicious, spiteful, or overbearing woman" and used informally and offensively "as a generalized term of abuse and disparagement for a woman." Sit with that for a moment. *Ouch*. Nobody wants that label as defined and intended thrown at them, let alone a woman leader.

When you look up *assertive*, it is "defined to act or characterized by bold or confident statements or behavior." Synonyms of *assertive* include *aggressive*, *ambitious*, *go-getting*, and *pushy*. Why are assertive women mislabeled as bitches? Because people don't always recognize the distinction that confidence and ambition, decisiveness and directness, aren't always complemented with malice or spite.

From the time I was a little girl, I was described as strong-willed, stubborn, and direct. Let's be honest: the terms *shy*, *wallflower*, and *quiet* were not descriptors teachers—or anyone else for that matter—used when referring to me. I knew what I wanted and had no qualms about advocating for it or working my butt off to accomplish it. I also recognized that not everyone possessed such a quality and would speak up for others and the injustices I witnessed. I have always been proud of my convictions. My mother, on the other hand? Let's just say there were times when she was flat-out embarrassed. Too many times to count, after I spoke up to someone or some injustice, my mother would exasperatedly exclaim, "I don't know where she came from!" While she's always been proud of who I am and what I've accomplished, she certainly distances herself from being responsible for my strong qualities. Why? Likely because of the negative connotation or bitch label that goes with it. Me, on the other hand? I never shy away from my strong-willed nature and the opportunity to speak up. I embrace who I am to the fullest.

While I could share stories all day long about being labeled a bitch for the times when I had to strongly and in no uncertain terms direct someone to take a specific action or to stand up for myself and be assertive to people trying to walk all over me, those are a dime a dozen and not my most teachable moments. The goodness in learning comes from stories and insights, where self-reflection leads us to change our perspective or viewpoint. I'll start back toward the beginning of my career when I first entered the workforce. At that time, I was eager to please and used my ambition and go-getter qualities in positive ways to demonstrate aptitude and competence to make things happen. I was always up to the challenge and quickly found my career on a fast, upward trajectory. It was only when I had "made it" and reached a pinnacle in my career and success that I realized the tipping point of going from the ambitious, go-getting, and assertive labels to being labeled a bitch. As I grew in my professional career, I found it increasingly more difficult to avoid the bitch label. Was it the position that I held that changed this label? It certainly wasn't that I changed the essence of who I am, so the only logical explanation I have uncovered is that it was a byproduct of circumstances.

Every day, leaders make decisions and direct people to take action. Decisiveness is an essential quality in leadership. I first assumed a leadership role within the government because I had grown in the organization and proven myself. When I became the boss, it wasn't my approach that changed but the expectations my employees had of me that changed. The challenge became aligning the expectations of others with my authentic self as a leader, and that is where the lesson lies. The people I was leading at the time were from various backgrounds, had distinctly different personalities all over the broad spectrum of personalities, and even varying levels of ambition. I was working in the government, and many folks had been there for years after working slowly up the ladder to the coveted GS-15 position, the highest level on the regular pay scale before the executive. Some were retired military who had sacrificed many years of service for our nation and were embarking on their "second" careers after reaching a high point of authority in their first career.

My authentic self as a leader is caring, flexible, and supportive while holding people accountable to the same quality standards, pressures, and capabilities I hold myself to performing daily. I saw myself as a balanced leader, after all, challenging and demanding but caring and flexible. I cared so deeply that my team had a good work-life balance that I chose to complete tasks I could easily do instead of delegating, so they were not stressed with reprioritizing work or extra burdens. To me, I was being a caring leader and saving them from stress. To them, I didn't trust them to complete work within their job duties.

I soon found that the qualities I expected from my team to match my strategic thinking, data analysis, and complex problem-solving capabilities needed improvement. How could that be? Our organizational name had the word *strategic* in it, yet several people lacked basic strategic thinking capabilities! I was shocked and needed to come up with a solution because that's the problem solver in me. Here I was as a new government leader, expecting carbon copies of myself to deliver strategic, high-quality, timely solutions. I wasn't going to change my expectations, so the solution needed to address the capability gaps. I decided that when the team fell short of the mark, I would help them develop these qualities since good leaders invest, coach, and develop their people. My tactic for developing the team was to provide many comments, edits, and explanatory directions to help the team achieve the level of perfection I sought. These comments needed to adequately explain my perspective and viewpoint so my team could gain meaningful insights, apply them to their work, and grow. Back then, comments were regularly handwritten on printed documents, and to add insult to injury, I chose to use a red pen to deliver my thoughts. To me, I was helping them grow and investing in them as any good leader would. To them, I was a bitch.

My intent wasn't malicious, and I honestly had no ill will in my actions. I was seeking to help our team succeed in meeting that high bar of perfection I had set. My feedback aligned with my authentic self, direct and to the point, and definitely not sugar-coated. The opposite of what I wanted to happen did—people gave up and felt defeated. They were not learning and growing from my shared insights but were shutting down. I couldn't understand why as I poured my heart and soul into developing people and the quality of our work products. I considered sharing the "why" behind an action or comment important, so that's exactly what I was doing in this process. Unfortunately, the "why" and insights were lost on the delivery.

I hate to admit it, but I took years to reflect on this situation and grow and learn from it as a leader. Years later, when someone asked me why I used a red pen and gave them comments like I was the teacher, I realized they felt scolded and unmotivated by my actions. Reflection has taught me that the team needed and expected me to adjust my delivery and style to accommodate their feelings, personality, and work style instead of applying a blanket approach that ultimately worked for no one. This realization goes against everything I was taught in high school, which was that in life, you must adjust to the teacher's (or in real life, to the boss') expectations to successfully deliver what they're looking for as they should not be the ones to adjust to you. Well, here I was, in the real world, being figuratively slapped across the face and informed that the boss needs to change their style to adjust to every individual to bring out the best in each of them. How profound.

The point is that the bitch label happens even without malicious intent, as it is all about how the person on the receiving end feels. My advice is to think about your delivery and ensure that it is known that you are coming from a place without malice or ill will. Remember, there are two sides to the story and different perspectives to consider, as the intent of your actions and words may not match how others perceive them.

I wish I could say that all my problems are solved, and I've never again encountered a situation where I'm labeled a bitch, but I can't and unlikely never will. I will always face these situations by being true to my authentic self at the core because of my directness and ambition. With intentional self-awareness, you (and I) can navigate these scenarios better and consciously work to adjust the approach, as appropriate, to reduce the likelihood it will be received as bitchy.

Tiffany

From the playground to the boardroom, women who assert themselves often find themselves unfairly labeled. The terms *bossy* and *bitch* seem to be the go-to descriptors for any woman who dares to speak her mind or take charge. Grab your popcorn and maybe a cocktail. I will share my journey of embracing that strength with a sprinkle of humor to highlight the absurdity of these stereotypes.

Picture this: fourth grade, a year filled with colorful lunch boxes, awkward clothes and hairstyles, and the sweet, naïve belief that if you work hard, you'll be rewarded. During this time, my teacher assigned captains for a class project. Naturally, I took the reins, guiding my team like a mini-CEO. But halfway through, my teacher started calling me bossy. Suddenly, *bossy* became my middle name, and my classmates were happy to tease me. I can still hear the echoes of their chants: "Bossy, bossy, bossy!" If only I'd known then, these were the early rumblings of leadership skills. Instead, it shattered my confidence, leaving me hesitant to voice my opinions for fear of the bossy label. It's funny now, looking back, how such a small word wielded such power over my young self.

Fast forward to my early college years, when group projects were a regular part of the curriculum. Most students did enough to get by, but I couldn't shake the habit of stepping up and taking the lead. Naturally, this often resulted in me doing the lion's share of the work. Did I ever confess this to my professors? No, because the fear of being labeled a bitch for speaking up was too great.

It's amusing in hindsight. Imagine me, the reluctant leader, always ending up as the project manager while silently cursing my assertiveness. Childhood fears have a funny way of tagging into adulthood, don't they? Yet, this phase was crucial. It taught me that it was not sustainable to hold back my true potential out of fear.

In my professional career, there were numerous instances where I had to be assertive, give directives, and make tough calls. Interestingly, my tone and body language were often critiqued as cold or harsh. Meanwhile, my male colleagues could yell and curse, only to be excused with comments like, "He's just having a bad day."

I will openly admit that after observing other strong, powerful women, I, too, adopted an aggressive and somewhat "bitchy" demeanor. I didn't know any other way until I met women who were just as powerful yet humble, kind, strong, and caring. Through these interactions, I realized authentic leadership doesn't require harshness. People are more likely to follow you when they feel supported and valued.

As I began incorporating these lessons into my leadership style, I noticed a significant shift in how others responded to me. Instead of leading with fear and intimidation, I started leading with empathy and encouragement. It was transformative. My team members felt more empowered, morale improved, and productivity soared. I learned that showing vulnerability and compassion didn't undermine my authority; it strengthened it.

Moreover, I discovered that creating a positive and supportive environment benefited my colleagues and enriched my professional and personal life. The energy I once spent maintaining a tough exterior was now channeled into building meaningful relationships and fostering a collaborative atmosphere.

One memorable incident was when I was promoted to senior vice president. My task was to improve margins on a specific contract. I worked with a director who questioned my every move, often bypassing me to go directly to the Chief Operating Officer. She even started spreading rumors that I was acting like a bitch. The irony was rich: me doing my job was more straightforward to label negatively than to acknowledge her insubordination.

A white woman was permitted to mistreat a Black supervisor/colleague, and after a year of enduring this disrespect, the white woman was eventually placed under new leadership. Reflecting on this situation, it's difficult not to conclude that if a Black woman had exhibited similar behavior toward her white supervisor, she would have faced much harsher consequences, possibly even termination. The double standards were glaringly evident.

African-American women face an even steeper climb. The "angry Black woman" stereotype looms large, forcing us to navigate our professional and personal lives with an added layer of caution. I remember practicing my speeches in the mirror, meticulously monitoring my tone, facial expressions, and body language. The mirror became my harshest critic, reminding me that any slip could reinforce an unfair stereotype.

Through this journey, I've understood that true power lies in lifting others, not pushing them down. By embracing a leadership style that combines strength and kindness, we can break the cycle of negative stereotypes and redefine what it means to be a powerful woman today. I've learned to embrace my strength and assertiveness. It's a delicate balance, challenging societal norms while staying true to myself. But it's crucial not to let society define us. We must challenge these preconceived notions and redefine what it means to be a robust and assertive woman.

To every young woman reading this, take time to understand yourself. Spend time alone, reflect on your actions, and ask yourself: *What do I want to be known for? What kind of leader, colleague, and person, do I aspire to be?* Building this foundation will help you mature and become the best version of yourself.

In times like these, humor and resilience are your best allies. Over the years, I've learned to appreciate a good laugh and not take things seriously. After all, work is not life, and we don't live to work. Embrace the absurdities and laugh at the stereotypes. The world is still learning to appreciate the depth of feminine power, and sometimes, the best way to cope with inequities is to find humor in the situation and remain resilient. By challenging societal norms and staying true to our values, we can reshape the narrative and be the strong, assertive women we were always meant to be.

Chapter 3:
Poor Behavior—How Women Treat Women

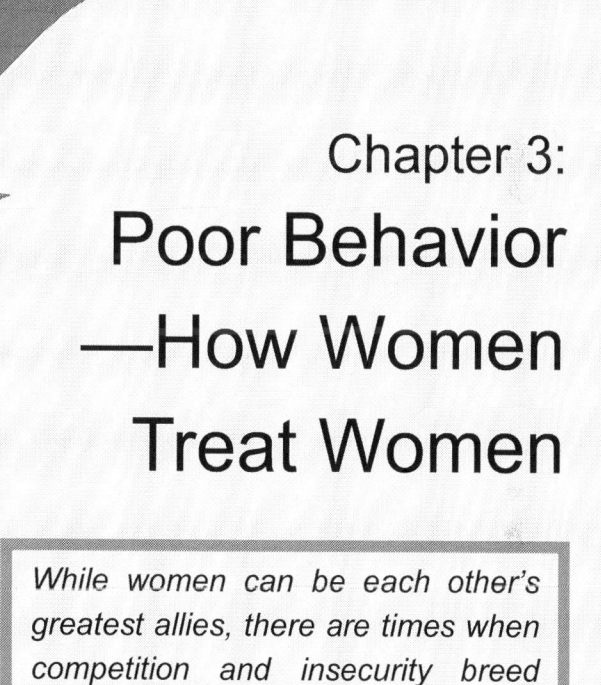

While women can be each other's greatest allies, there are times when competition and insecurity breed conflict. In this chapter, we explore the complexities of female dynamics in the workplace, sharing our experiences with jealousy, mistrust, and societal pressures. We also highlight the importance of fostering compassion, collaboration, and mentorship to lift each other up.

Helene

I have always loved the saying, "Do unto others as you would have them do unto you," also known as The Golden Rule. It is too bad that neither gender often follows it. But it seems even less followed between women, and for the life of me, I cannot figure out why. Is it jealousy? Is it insecurity? Is it cattiness? Is it competitiveness? Or a combination of it all? Whatever the reasons, I have never met anyone who has followed this rule consistently, myself included.

Why do women mistreat other women at times? Don't get me wrong; no one does this all the time. We can all be caring, supportive, warm, and pleasant, but sometimes, we cannot help ourselves.

When I think about the ways I have been treated throughout my career by other women, the actions I have experienced are backstabbing, game-playing, cruelness, and just plain meanness. As I stated earlier, I have been guilty of doing this at times as well. In my case, my poor behavior is based entirely on insecurity. My biggest flaw is having thin skin. I have always taken everything personally. I am convinced I know what everyone thinks, and I always go low. I am one of those half-empty-glass-of-water people, especially regarding people and how I am treated. As long as I can remember, I have been like this.

It started in my childhood when I was teased about how I looked, my faith, and how I did not fit the mold. I just never followed the crowd. The people who picked on me were both boys and girls, but it seemed the boys did it to my face, whereas the girls did it behind my back. My observation is that females behave poorly indirectly. That is why, growing up, I had very few girlfriends. I couldn't figure them out.

The boys were easy. They said what they thought to your face—no guessing needed. Plus, they said what they said and just moved on. They did not hold back or hold it in. They did not need to compete. They did not gossip. They went by the old WYSIWYG (what you see is what you get). I loved that! And I went by that as well. I just said what I thought to people's faces (just like the boys did, but no one called them a bitch). That way, I did not have to hold it in, and once I got things off my chest, I felt better. The problem is that people, especially girls, did not easily hear or accept my thoughts.

They never knew what I would say or if I would go off on them. They did not think I did this because I feared what people would say about me behind my back. I have had people do that my whole life, and I don't like it. I have always deflected arrows and was just plain scared of being attacked.

Fast forward to the changing moment—when I learned to be nicer. I once worked for someone who was constantly talking behind others' backs. This person was relentless. And I heard it all and let it happen. I thought that if it was not happening to me, I could protect the people being talked about and myself by ignoring him. It lasted a year until I could no longer stand it. It was just too cruel. So, I stood up for my peers, who were the victims of the behavior I always hated, and as you can guess, I fell into the same pothole as my peers. Well, that was it for me. It was like a lightbulb turned on. I realized that talking behind one's back and directly to one's face is equally damaging. After all, who is to say what you think of someone is right? Who is to say people need you to say what you think? And mostly, if I cannot handle someone telling me what is wrong with me, why do I think I have the right to tell them what is wrong with them?

The Golden Rule became real to me. I do not want to be told what is wrong with me—at least not what someone else thinks are wrong with me. Plus, I have no right to do that to others. And even though it can sometimes be fun to gossip behind someone else's back—to fit in and be part of the group—it is just wrong.

I try hard to keep my mouth closed. When I am so tempted to show how smart I am, how intuitive I am, or how, in my mind, I am looking out for others, I need to remind myself that it is a lousy idea. Am I perfect? No way! I can honestly say that I have done this in the past mainly because I wanted to be accepted, to be liked, and not to be hurt. But that is my issue, my insecurities—not theirs.

Before I close this chapter, I want to share another approach I have taken as I mature (age). In the past, when people hurt me, I sucked it up and took it. Not anymore. When I feel I've been treated poorly, I pack my bags and go home. That's right. I walk away from the person(s) who have caused me grief, and I do not choose to interact with them anymore. I do not choose to be anyone's target. I'm at the point in my life where if I take on a task and do not feel comfortable with whom I am working, I will leave that position instead, causing me unnecessary drama. It is better for my stress level and better for the organization.

So, my advice to readers is to think about others before you act. Remember, ladies, that watching someone else succeed does not reflect poorly on you. Helping others succeed is a great reflection on you. Talking behind someone's back sometimes feels good because it's fun to be accepted and feel like part of a group but consider how it would feel to be the victim of this or to have someone you care about be the victim. And lastly, no one is intuitive enough to know how and why others act. So, instead of sharing your unsolicited opinion, close your mouth and listen. You might learn something. Remember that the Golden Rule is a great way to live your life. If you do not want to be hurt, do not hurt others. Instead, treat others with understanding and care if you want to be happy, loved, and feel good about yourself. Then you will be rewarded, and you can be proud of you!

Linda

This chapter was difficult to write because of the pain of having women or even other Black folks turn on you or mistreat you. As professional women, we learn to let our light shine through a series of career successes. We are admonished not to hide our light under a basket.

Hiding our light under a basket deprives the world of our unique radiance. My talents, passions, and purpose are gifts that I am meant to share, not keep hidden out of fear or insecurity. When I allow my light to shine, I inspire others to do the same and create a ripple effect of positivity and empowerment. I still find it difficult to understand why others would want to invest so much of their time to extinguish the light of others, but they do.

A noteworthy "women against women" example happened when I was appointed to a Chief Information Officer role and asked to lead an organization where the morale was low and right after my predecessor reassigned the entire leadership team and hired new managers. Since I was in a science and technology organization, I had a particular interest in expanding the representation of women and helping their light to shine. I was meeting a resistance that was difficult for me to understand.

At the end of one frustrating workday, I discovered that someone filed a grievance against me based on these efforts. As the sun set and cars were steadily leaving the parking lot, I decided to pray (yes, prayer is a leadership tool!) about this latest dilemma. I wanted to understand *who* would do this. After I said my amens, someone walked through the door. I was surprised someone was still in the office. She walked up to me, wanted a hug, and kissed me on the cheek. Judas betrayed Jesus with a kiss. My Judas had now entered the scene. *Judas Number One.*

Judas Number One complained about something, but I had difficulty understanding what she was trying to say. Then, one of her buddies walked into my office. *Judas Number Two.* They both started a pity party about how hard things were for them. Judas Number Three was too scared to enter my office, but her cohorts made her case—my desire to help and be supportive triggered my empathy. However, I couldn't forget that Judas Numbers One, Two, and Three had just been revealed. As it turned out, they were indeed Judases. I tried to comfort them and perhaps did not do enough to help them. Nevertheless, they betrayed me by instigating trouble by filing grievances and complaints of discrimination.

Nearly twenty years later, the distance of time has calmed down my inner empath and the bitterness I harbored in that situation. Now, I can reflect on this situation with more clarity. Why would women turn against women? How can organizations address this? How can we battle this?

Create work environments that support women. Judas Numbers One, Two, and Three were Black women like me, yet they needed to compete with me to succeed. The Judases were not equipped to flourish in this kind of environment. Therefore, they chose me to sabotage. The Judases were equipped to affect behaviors that would gain them a slice of the best pound cake held back at church dinners (if you know, you know). It's too bad they couldn't use their pound cake skills for good.

Provide adequate support and mentorship. The Judases did not have anyone to advise and support them. They only had each other. This incestuous relationship created an echo chamber, only reinforcing their evil intent. They would have benefited from having relationships with mentors who would help them grow their networks and increase their skills. They needed a reliable network to socialize with and help them understand better ways to operate in a culture that valued competition versus collaboration.

Overcome gender bias and stereotypes. The organization and the Judases needed to learn to recognize and overcome unconscious biases and stereotypes that impact their perceptions and interactions. I understood what the Judases had to go through. Black women who raise their voices are accused of being bitches.

The bitch stereotype of Black women is a harmful and inaccurate portrayal of them, perpetuating discrimination and inequality. Historical stereotypes and biases increase the negative connotations of these traits for Black women. The "angry Black woman" trope portrays Black women as aggressive, confrontational, and irrationally angry, blaming their behavior on personal shortcomings rather than systemic obstacles. Media portrayals reinforce these stereotypes, shaping public opinion and promoting the idea that Black women's assertiveness is unfeminine or aggressive. To combat these stereotypes, it is crucial to highlight Black women's diverse experiences and contributions to society, as well as examine their biases and narratives.

I find it quite tempting to conform or downplay my abilities to avoid looking like a bitch or being threatening. Furthermore, I want to avoid conflict or making myself a target of woman-on-woman or Black-on-Black crime or the anti-diversity rope-a-dope (which sucks, by the way, but that's another book). It hurts to get attacked. Bottom line: Hiding my light doesn't protect me from any of this nor does it help other women. My advice is to use your light to help other women.

Jackie

Some of my biggest career champions have been women. On the contrary, some of my most prominent critics and backstabbers have been women. It can be so challenging to know when you're going to be back-stabbed because those same women will smile to your face and put on a good act. What I believe to be the number one reason for this behavior is simple: Some women cannot stand to see others succeed. This treatment pains me as someone who is direct and prides myself on not being two-faced.

You know the saying, "We're in a man's world?" Well, think about how cutthroat it can be to be a woman leader in this man's world. The scrutiny of being under a microscope and having every step watched as someone waits for you to falter is stressful. In this world, it is much more critical that we, as women, stick together in numbers to build each other up instead of cutting each other down.

I've experienced—too many times to count—interactions with women who are looking to burn you at any cost to help themselves get ahead. These women have terrible habits, with one common theme of being able to smile to your face while throwing you or your team under the bus in front of an audience. These women often thrive on publicly bringing up issues that are going on in the workplace that could quickly be resolved privately and politely. They resort to public shaming to get what they need while cutting you down to help them get ahead. They don't understand how valuable relationships are to getting things done effectively. Do you know what these women lack? They lack respect. If respect were present, they would pick up the phone, get on a video call, or even send a courtesy email asking for what they needed instead of resorting to the public-shaming approach. The funny thing is, people who witness this behavior aren't stupid, they see what it is at face value. In the process of showing their true colors, these back-stabbers burn bridges and coalitions much faster than they can build them. Respect is just as much something that is earned as it is received.

The lesson here is that no matter what, I try not to treat these women the same way. Am I always successful in taking my advice? No way! After all, I'm human and can only take so much fakeness. As executives—or at any level—we should work things out amongst ourselves. I send courtesy emails, pick up the phone or video call, and politely remind my colleagues who likely have fifty other things they're balancing that I need their input *before* ever resorting to public shaming. And if I need to bring up the status of something to the bosses or publicly, I politely say that we're still waiting for a couple of outstanding responses. Still, I do not call people out by name unless necessary. After all, you can't build bridges with fire!

Not every experience I've had in my career with women involves backstabbing; I've been fortunate enough to be surrounded by strong women leaders who have mentored me and nourished my career. One former colleague—a mentor and friend—has taken me under her wing because she believes in me. Her career spans many successful years as a government executive across the same department where I work. Now, in retirement, she has no tangible benefit from the mentorship and guidance she provides me. I know that she is one of my biggest champions but also the person who can give constructive advice and have hard conversations with me as I navigate my career. As a champion and mentor, she goes out of her way to make sure I am connected to other strong women leaders in my line of work and ensures opportunities for connecting with those leaders so that I can continue to grow and expand my network. She does this all because she firmly believes in women helping other women. Along the way in her career, she's had similar experiences of women supporting and helping her out, so she's giving back to me what was so generously given to her.

I've also worked to build my network of trusted women colleagues for whom I'll do anything short of breaking the law. We're here to build each other up, to support each other, and to provide the space and grace needed to vent. We have each other's backs, and with them, I never look over my shoulder for the dagger. I've embraced the women-supporting-women mantra. I've recently put myself out there to help two stellar female colleagues applying for senior executive service positions navigate the interview process and write their executive core qualifications. Did I have to help? No. Did I get anything tangible out of helping them? No. It was a rewarding opportunity for me to pay it forward and help build up other women. Although it only took a few hours of my time and effort to help, I know that the positive impact, morale boost, and kindness they felt in receiving my support couldn't be quantified.

Be the woman supporting other women; better yet, be the one helping others, period. In a world where negativity and competitiveness are the norm, we should work to normalize kindness and champion each other. Be authentically happy for someone else's success. Wouldn't you want the same? People remember how you made them feel above anything else. Simple acts of support, kindness, and lending a hand when someone needs it make a huge difference.

Tiffany

Have you ever seen the movie *Mean Girls*? Well, it exists in real life. Funny enough, I worked with a group of mean girls, and people just managed to stay out of their way. I recall an ex-colleague who faced significant issues with this group. Because she disagreed with them when they presented ideas or asked for recommendations, she was ostracized and placed on an "invisible island." Despite expressing her concerns to human resources, she eventually left the company. And don't get me started on human resources—rarely the advocate for the people like they're supposed to be.

I've been fortunate to have some great mentors who have opened doors and provided invaluable advice in my personal life and professional career. Sadly, there have been very few women among them. Why is it that some women aren't willing to help other women? Are they jealous? Do they feel threatened? What's going on? Women can be incredibly harsh toward one another, especially in a professional setting. We are quick to judge each other—whether it's your makeup (too much or not enough), your hair, your clothes, the way you talk, your kids, your spouse! We expect perfection from each other, but why?

I remember working with a woman who criticized everything I said and did early in my career. She made it her mission to find something wrong with every idea or recommendation I proposed. One day, she even went so far as to tell me to tone down my makeup to avoid looking like a clown. You must have tough skin in this game.

What does it mean to have tough skin? It means being resilient and handling criticism, rejection, or adversity without being easily hurt or offended. It has meant the ability to withstand negative comments or situations without letting them affect my emotional well-being.

Does this behavior stem from a fear of seeing others succeed, or does society condition us to put each other down and find fault before recognizing the good? I don't see men doing this as much. Instead of fostering collaboration, some women feel compelled to compete aggressively against one another, fearing that another woman's success could diminish their chances.

As a young woman, I found myself competing with other women and being a little catty but never a mean girl. It doesn't feel good to put another human being down, much less be part of a clique that operates like this. My "aha" moment came when I realized that uplifting each other is far more powerful than tearing each other down. In 2008, I joined an organization called Women in Technology, which was focused on empowering women in the technology and professional industries. I discovered that supporting and collaborating with other women could achieve more and create a more positive and productive environment. This shift in perspective improved my relationships with my colleagues and fostered a sense of community and empowerment that benefited everyone involved. Embracing this mindset has shown me the true strength of feminine power and the incredible things we can accomplish when we stand together.

As I've grown and matured in my career, I take the time to celebrate women every chance I get. What I've realized is that we are all struggling with some insecurity. A compliment and even words of encouragement are so important for women. We must learn to uplift one another. Maya Angelou said, "A person may forget what you said, but they will always remember how you made them feel."

We should support each other instead of succumbing to jealousy or competition. When we do, we create a stronger, more inclusive environment where everyone can thrive.

To the women who are new in their careers, here are some recommendations to foster a positive environment and avoid falling into the trap of harsh competition:

Celebrate other women. Make a conscious effort to recognize and celebrate the achievements of your female colleagues. A simple compliment or word of encouragement can go a long way.

Seek and offer mentorship. Sharing knowledge and experiences can help build stronger bonds and provide mutual support. While men can be great mentors, a woman-to-woman connection can feel particularly special. Find a mentor with experience and wisdom who can help you navigate challenges and champion your success. You need someone in your circle to say, in the words of former first lady Michelle Obama, "When they go low, we go high," and you also need someone to say, in the words of my sister Erica Cook, "When they go low, we go lower."

Focus on collaboration over competition. Working together leads to better outcomes and a more positive work environment. Encourage teamwork and collective success.

Be mindful of your words. Avoid making judgmental or critical comments about another woman's appearance, choices, or abilities. Instead, offer constructive feedback when appropriate. Remember, it's hard enough at times to find the strength to face the day. Practicing positive habits, like starting your day with affirmations, can set a positive tone. It starts with you!

Affirmations

- Why not me?
- You are smart enough.
- You will succeed in everything you do.
- You are beautiful.
- You are worthy of greatness.
- You are fierce, and so is the circle of women around you.

Build a supportive network. Cultivate relationships with supportive colleagues and friends who can offer advice, encouragement, and assistance when needed.

Chapter 4:
Big Girls Do Cry

> Tears are often perceived as a sign of weakness, yet we believe they are a powerful expression of strength and humanity. In this chapter, we share our stories of vulnerability, resilience, and emotional authenticity. Together, we uncover why embracing our emotions, rather than suppressing them, is a vital part of leadership and personal growth.

Helene

There is nothing more exhausting yet cleansing than a good cry. I am not talking about weeping when watching a movie and the dog gets hurt. I am not talking about crying when you kiss your loved one goodbye at the airport and then return to your car. I am talking about the cry where you need tissues, one where you must excuse yourself so you can get your act together. You know what I mean—a big ugly cry.

I feel bad for someone who cannot cry. How do they keep all that inside? We have all heard the saying, "Big boys/girls don't cry." Or my favorite, "Put your big girl panties on and get over it." What a pile of malarkey!

I say, go ahead, let it out! You will feel better. Crying will clear your mind so you can figure things out. You will signal the need for comfort from your family, friends, or peers. In other words, you must let it out to bounce back.

Now that's all fine and good when you are home with family or out with friends, but what about at work? I admit I am a crier. The tears well up in my eyes, my nose gets red, and I cannot hide it and stop it. I do not cry immediately, of course. But there was *that* situation when I heard these words from a superior or human resources at work—yes, the old "Can I see you in my office?" That was when my panic set in. It could be good news. It could be news about someone else. Or it could be news about the company, who knows. My immediate thoughts were, *What did I do or say to cause this meeting?* I immediately went into fight-or-flight mode. Heart racing, increased breathing, nervousness. Somehow, I managed to get into their office (unless they wanted to torture me and make me wait until later in the day or the next day) and sat down and waited. I knew immediately whether it was bad news for me. If not, everything came to a halt—no more panic. My heart rate and breathing slowed down, and I immediately relaxed. I was ready to receive and discuss the news. But if it was even the tiniest bit about me (perceived or not), tears came to my eyes. The tears did not necessarily mean I was sad, especially at work. I cannot remember a time that I cried out of sadness unless it involved someone being ill or passing away. Most of the time, the tears were from anger or outrage. And that, my friends, is where the rubber hits the road. *I did not want to cry!* I wanted to keep my face neutral, showing interest in hearing more. But what I wanted and what happened were not always in line.

My suggestion if you find yourself in a fight-or-flight situation or need a good cry—whether out of anger, anxiety, fear, or sadness—is to go to a safe place where you are free to let it out and have a good cry. If you have a mentor or friend you can trust not to break your confidence, bring them with you. Then, wait until you are calm and can compose yourself, and then, if possible, get away from the situation for a bit. Go for a walk, go home, do whatever is practical, and take a break. A walk helps me clear my mind and think things through. Others meditate, take deep breaths, or do whatever works for them.

Many companies offer counseling benefits if you want help. If you have a behavior that you do not wish to continue, do not ignore it. Leverage the advice of experts. Find a way to change. It may be crying, anger, insecurities, or substance issues. Whatever you are experiencing that you cannot change on your own, do not just try to compensate or ignore it. Also, holding it in is not a good option—trust me.

This is one area where I can say, "Do as I say, not as I do." Since I cried at work, I may not be the best woman to give advice. I will encourage you to do what's best for you. If you want or need to cry, grab some tissues and go for it.

Linda

I played the French horn in high school—at Duke Ellington School of the Arts in Washington, D.C. As music majors, we were required to give a recital on our instrument each year. I played a concerto and was accompanied by my piano teacher. When I performed, I hit a wrong note, which is easy to do on the French horn, then I freaked out and got nervous. With each note I played, you could hear the quiver. I cried. Tears just streamed down my face until I got so upset I ran off the stage. My sixteen-year-old self was mortified. My band teacher comforted me and said I sounded good; he wanted me to play for the Parent Teacher Association (PTA). So, I did it, hitting the same wrong note. I got nervous again and started crying, but this time, I played through the tears.

As I traversed my Information Technology (IT) career, I swore I would never let them see me cry. I was meeting at a law enforcement organization early in my executive career. I was criticized and humiliated in the meeting, but I didn't cry... I stood tall and took the bullets. On my way home, I called my husband and told him I had a bad day and needed a Cosmopolitan. I pulled the car in the garage, barely managing not to T-bone the freezer, which was strategically placed where I parked. I could hear the martini shaker through the garage door. I took a sip and started crying ugly tears. My heart was broken, and my soul weakened. Nevertheless, I dried my tears and faced those law enforcement executives the next day, with a stronger heart and a rejuvenated soul.

I had a pretty good mastery over the tears until I was in a so-called training session on race, power, and privilege. We did what the facilitator called a Privilege Walk. It highlighted that while everyone had some privileges, some had significantly more than others. I was in the back of the room with the less privileged folks, clearly and distinctly separated from my non-Black colleagues. It hurt to be in the back of the room. All I could do was cry. I was inconsolable in a room full of my peers. As it turned out, my tears affected them. It didn't matter; it hurt so much, and it still does.

The following week, one of my work buddies who missed the meeting must have heard something and asked me how it went. I told him, but he was British and didn't get this American race nonsense, so I cried in front of him, and he told me what I needed. I looked at him puzzled, and he said, "Peking duck. I will pick you up in five minutes." We went to this excellent restaurant for lunch and had Peking duck and some wine, maybe a few bottles.

In retrospect, here is my advice:

Learn how to understand and manage your emotions. Are you crying from anger? Sadness? Fear? A mature leader needs to be able to self-regulate their emotions. Pay attention to yourself and understand the triggers. Reflect on some of your anger or crying episodes and consider alternate responses. As a musician, I learned to take a beat and then respond. You could also take a deep breath. I was in a situation where, with clarity and purpose, I decided to cuss out the deputy secretary of the Department of Energy. I took a deep breath to get everything out without breathing. My (male) deputy interrupted me (again) to express his (who cares?) opinion. This interruption gave me more beats and time to reconsider an alternative approach. After a few breaths, I used my anger to frame a better response. I turned my rage into courage and shared my opinions for the next steps.

Know yourself and be authentic. I was always reluctant to play into the stereotype of the angry Black woman. So often, we contort ourselves into pretzels to fit in. I'm not going to lie: fitting in is essential. But losing yourself won't work in the long run. I finally decided that it was acceptable for me to wear braids in a professional setting (perhaps we should have had a whole chapter dedicated to hair). This decision was…liberating. However, I am not naïve enough to think that people don't form decisions about you based on your hair, so, I got a wig—just in case.

Have a friend at work. Having someone in the room with you who understands you and knows how to keep you grounded is helpful. I was leading a particularly contentious meeting. Someone challenged me and asked me (out loud), *Who do you think you are?* I took a beat (learned that trick in the high school band) and asked her to repeat the question. I replied. Later that day, I had lunch with some girlfriends; one of them was in this meeting with me. Our crew laughed because she told them I answered the question, "I don't think, I know that I'm the CIO b***ch!" What I <u>actually</u> said was, "I am *THE* Chief Information Officer of The National Aeronautics and Space Administration's Goddard Space Flight Center." My girlfriend retorted, "Like I said, I'm the CIO b**ch!"

I cannot advise those of you early in your career to go ahead and cry, nor can I honestly say that stifling tears is always the best thing to do. But if all else fails, there is always Peking duck.

Jackie

Crying and showing emotion is healthy, but it should be done privately. Sometimes, nothing makes me feel better than just crying it out into my pillow at home. Crying can be attributed to sadness, fear, anger, happiness, stress, or exhaustion. I despise crying at work. Maybe it's because I'm a perfectionist and want to be viewed as having everything together. Perhaps it's because there's never a tissue in sight when I need it most to wipe the snot running out of my nose and the tears streaming down my face. Maybe it's because—I'll say it—I'm an ugly crier! No matter the hundred reasons as to why I despise crying at work, tears sometimes cannot be stopped.

I have had several standout moments in my career when I cried that I will never forget. It isn't because I cried that these are engraved in my memory—it is because of how I felt in each situation. Some of these scenarios center around people striving to make me feel less than them in some way at important highlights in my career. Looking back now, it seems jealousy could have been a factor, but whatever it was, they took prime opportunities where I had career accomplishments to cut me down, and how I was treated overshadowed times that should have been a celebration that I can never get back. To this day, I can cry just thinking of what has been "stolen" from me in these very moments. I can still feel rage and frustration at my very core. What got me through these times was a couple of trusted colleagues.

They picked me back up, helped me dry my tears, and reassured me that my perspective of the situation wasn't wrong.

Back in the early years of my life the perfectionist in me strived to deliver exceptional work products. I saw what I offered as a true reflection of myself and my capabilities, so nothing less than perfect would do for me. Well, we all know no one is perfect. It was a painful lesson to learn along the way, especially during my journey when constructive feedback was given. I took it personally. Growing up in school, I always strived to get straight A's. I took pride in mastering whatever subject I was learning and acing tests with limited study time or preparation. In the sixth grade, I was really enjoying my American History class and knew I was doing well. Before each quarter, my teacher would call each student up to the front of the class and discretely show what grade we would receive. When I was called to the front, the teacher showed me an "F". I immediately started crying in front of the class. The teacher felt horrible as he thought I would know it was a joke. Even knowing that I was averaging 98%, at that moment, the horror of potentially receiving an "F" crushed the perfectionist within me, and the tears could not be controlled. When I run into my teacher to this day, as I often see him when I'm back home in Rhode Island, he still shares this story and we both look back and chuckle about it now.

Early in my career, it was difficult to carry the weight of criticism because of how hard I worked toward perfection. Carrying the burden of being a perfectionist is a book in and of itself. Separating yourself from your work is tricky, especially for someone like me who puts such passion into it. It took years of growth and quite a few tears to understand that in most circumstances, the outcome, product, or situation is being criticized and can be enhanced. While I've spent years fighting my inner perfectionist to disassociate feedback from personal attacks, I owe it to my perfectionism that I've been able to turn these moments into something positive. I have been good at bottling up the energy I felt receiving such feedback and working hard to prove someone wrong or to deliver something better the next time. The hurt, anger, and frustration have proven in many ways to be a key ingredient in some of my most successful career moments. There's nothing more powerful than a woman with a point to prove!

When I've cried at work or in work-related settings, it was mainly brought on by sheer anger and frustration. You see, it takes quite a bit to get me to the point at work where I shed tears. I've grown thicker skin with age, but situations will still bring me to tears.

I can't say I've always been successful, but in maybe ninety percent of the instances of work crying, I've been able to do so privately or with a limited audience of trusted colleagues. The very stigma of being labeled as a crybaby, weak, or even too emotional is enough, in most cases, to deter me from tears. But I find that the tears that come with rage and frustration cannot be controlled.

Why are we labeled in such a negative way for expressing ourselves? With the current emphasis on mental health and wellbeing, shouldn't there be more grace? Unfortunately, that's not the case. In the workplace, I've heard everything from "suck it up, buttercup" to "I can't deal with this drama" from men who are speaking of women, specifically those who show emotion. I have seen firsthand women who are on the verge of getting emotional, trying to remove themselves politely from the situation only to be ridiculed and publicly shamed for crying.

Whatever comes out in emotion from the depths within and manifests as tears is authentic and raw. I have witnessed both men and women crying at work. We all need a safe place and trusted colleagues to confide in to help us through challenging times, so I don't take that role lightly if I find myself in it. Granted, I try to provide comfort first and then bring in humor, if appropriate, to get a chuckle and bring someone out of the moment. If someone comes to me in tears, I immediately try to find a private place to go if we aren't in one already. We've all seen situations where someone is shedding tears, and people show up in masses to provide comfort, all while drawing more attention to the poor person crying who likely wants to crawl into a hole. Someone with snot running out of their nose, bright red cheeks and eyes, and streams of tears hitting their clothing doesn't need a spotlight! Be there to comfort someone in their time of need but be just as prepared to step away from them if asked.

The big lesson here is not that you shouldn't cry; it's that once you're done crying, adjust your crown and put that emotion to good use. There will be people and circumstances that make you angry, frustrated, and sad, so take a moment to reflect on how you can come out of the situation positively and grow. Not every situation lends itself to tears, either. Grow a thick-skinned understanding that criticism isn't always personal and that sometimes the truth hurts. And when you need to cry it out, cry privately and try not to make a spectacle of yourself in front of the masses.

Tiffany

Have you ever seen a man cry in the workplace? If you have, I bet you can count the times on one hand. Is it because men don't cry? Hell no! They cry—they do it differently. Society, however, has conditioned us to believe that tears have no place in the professional world, especially when it comes to women.

Women are expected to embody strength, stoicism, and resilience without ever shedding a tear, as if emotion and capability are opposites. But let me tell you, I've cried. Oh, I've cried—mostly behind closed doors, where no one could see, because I thought showing emotion meant showing weakness.

Take 2002, for example. I was working at a prestigious bank and had recently been promoted. One afternoon, I was in the copier room—you remember those, right? While making copies, a colleague walked in, slapped me on the butt, and said with a straight face, "How's the day going?"

I froze—shocked, offended, and unsure how to react. Why didn't I address it right then and there? Maybe I didn't want to appear weak. Perhaps I didn't want to risk being labeled as "difficult."

The next day, I mustered the courage to go to human resources—you know how I feel about HR by now. The specialist promised, "We'll investigate and follow up." A week went by. No follow-up. When I went back to request an update, I was blindsided. The specialist told me, "We've received a complaint that you sexually harassed a colleague."

My mind reeled. Earlier that day, I'd told a colleague, "You look nice." That innocent compliment had somehow morphed into a harassment claim against me. The irony was suffocating. I went straight to my car and cried. I sobbed.

Sitting there, I felt powerless and unprotected. Reality hit me like a tidal wave, and I was expected to navigate a minefield where even advocating for myself could backfire.

In a world that expects women to wear the armor of invincibility, tears are often perceived as a weakness in that shield. But here's the truth: tears are not a sign of weakness. They are a testament to our humanity, a release of the pressure we carry, and a reminder of our strength.

Fast-forward a few years. I was a senior leader on a five-year program, working at a client site. Despite my title, I often found myself sidelined in meetings. One day, after being repeatedly talked down to, I had enough. I excused myself and walked to my car.

The moment I sat down, the dam broke. Tears streamed down my face, carrying the weight of frustration, exhaustion, and sheer emotional fatigue. As I cried, I glanced in the rearview mirror. My makeup was ruined and smeared. The raw emotion made it clear that something had to change. But I had a decision to make.

I wiped my tears, reapplied my lipstick, and looked at myself in the mirror. "Pull it together," I told myself. Or, as my co-author would say, "Put on your big girl panties." And I did.

I walked back into that building, not because I felt like it, but because resilience demanded it. This time, I was intentional. I didn't just sit quietly, waiting for my turn to speak. I leaned in literally and figuratively. I made eye contact, asked pointed questions, and asserted my expertise with confidence. When my ideas were dismissed, I redirected the conversation back to my points with data and strategic insights. Instead of letting others dominate, I facilitated discussions, ensuring my voice was not just heard, but respected.

I called out moments of condescension with professionalism, saying things like, "I'd like to build on that, but let's ensure we're looking at the full scope of the issue." I leveraged allies in the room, drawing them into the dialogue and reinforcing key messages. Most importantly, I stopped waiting for permission to lead, I took up space, owned my role, and commanded the room in a way that left no doubt about my value.

That day, I learned something critical: resilience isn't just about bouncing back, it's about showing up differently, with purpose, power, and presence.

Over the years, I've cried less. Maybe time and experience have hardened me, or maybe I've learned to channel my emotions differently. It's sad but true. Still, I wish someone had told me earlier in my career that strength doesn't mean holding it all in.

I've learned that resilience isn't about being unshakable; it's about rising after you've been shaken. It's about allowing yourself to feel deeply and authentically while knowing you'll emerge stronger on the other side.

If I could offer one piece of advice, it would be to embrace your emotions. Journal your feelings—write down what brought you to tears and how you processed those moments. Acknowledge your vulnerability because it's a powerful part of what makes you human.

Meditation, too, has been a lifeline for me. When emotions run high, find a quiet space—a restroom, a corner office, even your car. Close your eyes, breathe deeply, and let yourself reset. Walk it out if you need to. Something about the rhythm of your steps clears your mind and lightens your spirit.

Tears don't make you weak; they make you whole. They remind you that while you may bend under the weight of life's challenges, you will not break. You'll bounce back—stronger, wiser, and more resilient each time.

So, to all the "big girls" out there, let's rewrite the script. Big girls don't just cry, they cry, rise, and conquer.

Chapter 5: Mansplaining

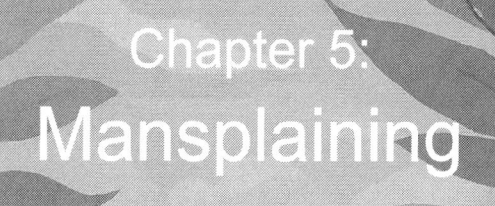

As women leaders, we often face the challenge of having our expertise questioned or our voices diminished. In this chapter, we take a candid look at the phenomenon of mansplaining and its impact on our professional spaces. Through our experiences, we explore strategies for reclaiming authority, asserting expertise, and fostering equitable communication.

Helene

Let me start with a couple of definitions. I looked these up because I wanted to be sure I was addressing the right issue. I could have asked the man sitting next to me as I wrote this chapter, and I'm sure he would have told me his definition. Instead, Googling it was much quicker, easier, and probably more accurate—if you catch my drift.

Mansplaining means to explain something to a woman in a condescending, overconfident, and often inaccurate or oversimplified manner, typically to a woman already knowledgeable about the topic. Mansplaining occurs when one party behaves as the default expert on a subject, regardless of the other party's expertise, experience, or body language.

This is a real problem for me. I do hate when men mansplain to me or other women. I find myself very impatient. This happens so often in my life. Whether it is asking where we are going or why something is done a certain way, most men must go into so much detail to answer. I want to say, "I'm not dumb! Just give me the answer. If I knew the answer, I wouldn't ask the question." Not only do they go into a ton of detail that I don't need, but they tend to dumb it down for me. I'd rather not know the answer than ask the question. Thank goodness for Google, Siri, and my new favorite, ChatGPT. And then there's the situation where someone asks me a question or for my opinion. Before I can open my mouth, a man who is suddenly the expert (in his mind) blurts out an answer. It is as if I am not the person they asked in the first place.

I can't tell you how often some man has cut me off to answer a question asked of me. If I take the time to formulate my response, I get cut off. I find my mouth open, and someone else's voice comes out of it, and that voice is usually lower in pitch and louder than mine. There I am, mouth open, and I'm giving the death stare to the man who is mansplaining the answer. In my head, my reaction is comprised of screams, telling him, "Shut up! They asked me! I can answer that!" Not to mention, the man who is answering often needs to be corrected. Then, I'm trying to figure out what to do. Do I correct him, or do I just let it go? Then there's the case when he repeats what I just said and takes credit for my thoughts and ideas. Again, the screams in my head occur, and I want to say, "I just said that! Are you kidding?" I guarantee if I said that, I would come off as a bitch.

So, there you go. I can relate to this in both my professional and personal life. I need a better way to handle this. I have tried many things. I have tried to cut the man off, but that doesn't usually work. I have tried to state the obvious—as in, excuse me, but I was asked the question. Again, that makes me look bad. I have tried to talk over the man. Not a good look. And I have tried to swallow my pride and let the man take credit for my ideas. That works, but it's so frustrating. The one helpful solution I have found is to let the man mansplain it wrong and look bad. That gives you a temporary good feeling, but in the end, it's frustrating because your silence may seem like you agree with the incorrect information. And if you care about the man, you feel bad for allowing them to lose credibility. Another way I have handled the group setting situation where a man repeats what I have said to get credit for his brilliance, is to be the first to shout out, "I agree, great idea (insert his name)." Those who have been paying attention will get a good chuckle. Those who were not may think you are such a team player, and in the end, your idea is recognized and perhaps implemented. I must say that I will discuss with the culprit who took my idea as his own after the meeting and let's say I will express how unhappy I am, and he will surely get an earful.

I do want the reader to know that you are not alone here. Mansplaining is alive and well in my world; unfortunately, it does not improve with age. Men need to be seen as relevant and experts when they age, which happens much more often. On the good side, as women age, many of us don't care as much. We know what we know and can quickly get up and walk away when a man mansplains to us or for us. And if the men around me want to show how brilliant they are and if they are wrong in their information, it's their problem to overcome. This is one of those situations in which age works better for women. Just make sure you walk away. You don't want people to think you agree with the mansplaining culprit. And eye rolling when he's speaking can help make light of an uncomfortable situation.

Linda

Mansplaining is a condescending or patronizing way a man explains something to a woman, assuming she lacks knowledge or expertise. It stems from gendered power dynamics and can perpetuate gender inequality by undermining women's contributions. The female professional must recognize and put strategies to address this behavior in her bag of tricks.

On the subject of mansplaining, I am reminded of actor and comedian Chris Tucker's iconic line, "Do you understand the words that are coming out of my mouth?" Working in a male-dominated field, as I have, has this phrase echoing around my head. I want to say that as you mature in your career, you won't see it anymore, but alas, you will. You can even get mansplained by another woman (and no this is not contradictory)!

I am a board member of a nonprofit organization with a great mission. There was a management issue that had elevated to an email conversation. I weighed in on the issue and sparked an outrageous reply from another woman telling me that I probably didn't have the management experience to understand the intricacies of the situation. *Whew!* I ate her up politely and professionally...I think. Her apology was almost as bad as the original sin. She didn't know I had the background she thought I didn't have. My standard answer these days is, "Google me," though I was thinking, *Google me, bitch.* I will stipulate that saying, "Google me, bitch," while internally satisfying, is not the best response. Here are three tips for getting through a mansplaining situation:

Stay calm and use humor. As a chief information officer, I had a male scientist throw a quarter at me and say, "Here's all we need for a terabyte of email storage (from Amazon)." I threw it back at him and said, "Clearly you haven't considered security which adds another 10 cents, plus we have 100,000 users so you can keep your quarter."

Engage in constructive interactions. Sometimes, I will say that *I just said the same thing.* What was it about how what I told you that sounded different? And I will insist on an answer. Try to use it to grow relationships and improve communication.

Call it out. Point out this behavior when it happens to others, especially from other women. Be respectful to other women so that the organizational culture does not feel it appropriate to treat them this way.

Oh, and one more: **Find your voice.** Finding your voice is a personal journey that requires acknowledging and following your intuition, reflecting on your values and beliefs, practicing self-expression, surrounding yourself with supportive people, embracing vulnerability, and seeking guidance from mentors or coaches. These steps help align your voice with what truly matters to you and help you connect with others on a deeper level. I am grateful that I have been able to reap the benefits of a good education in a safe environment where I could be brilliant, speak up, and share my thoughts. I was taught early on to find my voice.

Jackie

There's a pandemic facing corporate America, and the person who finds a cure will undoubtedly be a hero to many. I'm not talking about the COVID-19 pandemic that we just endured, but the kind that is impacting only the male gender. Mansplaining. Admittedly, the entire male species does not suffer from this ailment. The root of the issue is that for whatever reason, some men generally do not believe women are of equal or (God-forbid) superior intelligence, so they go to great lengths to break things down into lengthy explanations to (over)compensate for a woman's perceived lack of intelligence.

As a woman, once you start to recognize this behavior, it starts to annoy the hell out of you. Again, let me foot-stomp that mansplaining isn't a problem with all men, but in my life experiences, it has been pervasive in my career with many men. I've tried to rationalize the behavior by creating excuses for it in my mind. First, I blamed it on men with military or law enforcement backgrounds. Not to offend anyone in the military or law enforcement, I've just encountered too many men in my career who have an inferiority complex with such backgrounds and have correlated it to justify the mansplaining. Women leaders in the military and law enforcement are rare, which may explain why these men feel they had to mansplain.

Next, I chalked it up to age and generational gaps as it seems many of the mansplaining I've encountered were from old(er) men. My logic here ties back to my grandfather, who recently passed at the age of ninety-eight and was one of the best story tellers I knew. He provided excellent detail when painting a picture to tell his stories. Along the journey, he ensured the audience understood what he was describing or the topic of discussion. Could the mansplaining I endure in the office be tied to age? My grandfather certainly wasn't mansplaining; he was consciously trying to speak to people with differing backgrounds and knowledge of the topics being discussed to build an inclusive conversation. Is that the intent of these older men, but they're not great at doing so without coming across as insulting one's intelligence?

Let's face it: old, young, military/law enforcement background or not, the only excuse I can rationalize is that this is the male species' way of proverbially pounding their chests to demonstrate dominance and power in their intellect. Again, not all men suffer from this pandemic, and not all go around beating their chests to establish dominance. So, let me just call it what it is—a personality flaw. Bottom line: There is *no* excuse for this behavior.

So the big question is: What do I do, and how do I handle this in my career? The answer isn't quite simple. It depends on my mood, the day, and the audience. Each day, I have a lower tolerance for it. I have recently started calling this behavior out. For instance, I've had men briefing me on policies and explaining the guidelines and requirements around them. Poor fools don't realize that I was the one who wrote these policies and intimately know the rules, guardrails, and where the gray area exists between the words. I've used these circumstances to publicly share real-time feedback that I receive as mansplaining and that they should be careful how they come across. Was this effective? No. But did I feel better? Yes!

I've experienced the pain of interacting with men at work who mansplain every time we meet, to the point where other female colleagues would send me a note and say, "Didn't you just say that?" My approach has recently been to smile and respond with "That's a great idea" or "Good thought." This approach has served me well over calling out mansplaining for multiple reasons: One, I'm not embarrassing the person or publicly shaming them for this behavior (even though I desperately desire to); two, I recognize a good idea or thought when I hear one—whether or not it was something I said two minutes prior; and three, if we're working together in any capacity, the successful accomplishment of goals comes with collaboration, not pissing contests.

Whether you've encountered mansplaining or not up to this point in life, I can assure you that you will at some point. And once it happens, you may question whether your delivery or communication was clear and compelling. You may start reflecting on why men think that you don't have technical credibility and know things. You will suffer from questioning so much of yourself and your approach without realizing it's not you; it's them. So, I advise you to keep your chin up, smile graciously, and rise above it. You cannot prevent or stop this behavior, but you can control your reaction.

Tiffany

I'm trying to figure out what's worse: not being heard or repackaging your ideas in real time by a man who seems to think he was hired as your interpreter. This phenomenon, where a man explains something to a woman—often in a condescending or overbearing way—has earned the term *mansplaining*. And while the term points to men, let's be honest: women can and do engage in this behavior too. The kicker? Most people don't even realize they're doing it.

In my experience, some men seem to talk to hear their voices. Don't believe me? Try sitting in a meeting with a group of men. It's easy to spot the quiet ones who, ironically, often have the most to say. But then there are the others—the men who go out of their way to inflate their intellect, especially in the presence of women.

Working in information technology (IT), I've had my fair share of encounters with mansplaining. Perhaps it stems from stereotypes about gender and technical skills, or maybe it's simply because women only make up twenty-five percent of the IT workforce. The number drops even lower to just twenty percent at the executive level. That means you're likely to find only one woman in a room of five decision-makers.

Meeting after meeting, I've seen this pattern play out. I'll share a fully formed, well-thought-out idea only to have a male colleague repeat it moments later, slightly rephrased, and suddenly it's genius. The voice inside me screams, *I just said that!* But no one ever chimes in with, "Actually, that was her point." Instead, the conversation moves on as though my contribution was a mere placeholder for his revelation.

Mansplaining isn't just a term—it's an experience that reverberates in boardrooms, classrooms, and conversations across the globe. It's not about malicious intent; it's about a deeply ingrained dynamic where women's expertise is undermined, their voices drowned out, and their insights swept aside. Nothing stings more than a man assuming the role of narrator for experiences he hasn't lived, work he hasn't done, and perspectives he hasn't earned.

One moment stands out in sharp relief. During a high-stakes meeting about the company's strategy to expand our capabilities, I presented a bold plan to move into the data space. I outlined the risks, the precautions we'd need to take, and the innovative solutions that could set us apart. Heads nodded, and I thought, *Finally, they're listening.*

But as soon as I finished, one of the male executives leaned forward with that signature "let me break this down for you" expression and said, "What Tiffany's trying to explain is..." He then restated my entire plan, word for word, as if it had just materialized in his head. The frustration bubbled up inside me as I watched others nod along and even build on "his" points.

Was it my delivery? Did I need to project more authority? Or was this just a classic case of what many women experience in the workplace? My inner voice shouted, *I just said that!* But instead of snapping, I bit my tongue, choosing composure over confrontation.

Here's the truth: I don't think most men who do this are intentionally dismissive. Some might even think they're being helpful, but the impact is the same. Mansplaining diminishes women's contributions, reinforces inequality, and creates a culture where our voices don't carry the weight they deserve.

This isn't about villainizing individuals but dismantling the unspoken assumptions that fuel these behaviors. It's about redefining how we give credit where it's due and fostering a culture where ideas stand on their own merits, free from unnecessary reinterpretation.

If I could go back twenty years, I'd tell my younger self to advocate for her ideas and speak up for her colleagues because the truth is silence only perpetuates the problem. Owning your voice and claiming your space isn't just an act of defiance—it's a declaration of worth.

To the women reading this: Your voice is not inconvenient, your ideas are not a threat, and your contributions are not up for reinterpretation. Recognize the power within your words and the strength in your lived experiences. Mansplaining isn't a reflection of your inadequacy; it's a symptom of societal imbalance, and we're here to correct it.

Let's not forget the importance of supporting each other. If you witness a colleague being sidelined, speak up, call out the behavior, and advocate for one another. Together, we can create workplaces that amplify women's voices.

It's time to rewrite the narrative—one conversation, one meeting, one bold voice at a time.

Chapter 6: Finding Balance

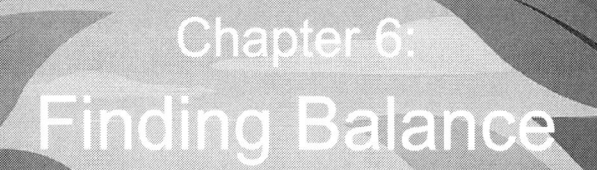

The pursuit of balance between career ambitions, personal passions, and family responsibilities is a challenge we all understand. In this chapter, we reflect on our struggles and share the strategies we use to juggle multiple roles. Together, we redefine what balance means, exploring how it evolves and how to create harmony on our own terms.

Helene

Finding balance is an exciting concept. How often have you been told you must take care of yourself? Which part of yourself? The first thing that comes to most women's mind is weight. We are either too skinny, too heavy, or somewhere in between. I can't count how many times I have gone through the following scenario. On Mondays, I go on a diet, exercise, and eat at home more often with the "right" food. Monday goes well. Tuesday goes well. Wednesday, there's an all-day meeting, and we are bringing in pizza or boxed lunches (with a cookie, of course), and then there's the three o'clock snack of brownies or chips. I'm skipping dinner since I'm exhausted. Oh no, Thursday comes along. I have a business lunch, and we are all working late on a proposal. Pasta and salad are brought in, along with cheesecake. Friday morning comes, and there's an all-hands with donuts for everyone. Oh well, I'll go out for a team lunch of Chinese food. Friday night is dinner out with the family. Oh wait, I forgot to exercise! I will walk an hour each day over the weekend to make up for each day missed during the week. Oh wait, there's kids' soccer and date night on Saturday. Sunday is football with all the goodies. I will start tomorrow—Monday—for real! However, I leave on Tuesday to travel to a conference. *Ugh*. I give up!

Okay, I will work on my mental health. One word here: *stress*. Work stresses us out. The people, the deadlines, the drive for profit, budgeting to meet your salary, and short- and long-term goals. Home is more stressful. I'm single and need to go out and socialize. I'm married and need to maintain that relationship. The kids—should we have some, and will they be happy and healthy if we do? Then there's the guilt of being a working mom. Will my kids turn out okay? Will they resent me? Am I a bad mom…and on and on.

As a woman, you can indeed have it all. But what does that mean? Can you excel at work? Can you be a good spouse, a good mom, a good friend, and a good daughter? Can you meet your goals? Do you have goals? I have two words for you: absolutely yes! With one caveat: you must have goals. You must have short-term goals (for the next five years) and long-term ones (throughout your career and onward). Do they have to be set in stone? Absolutely not! However, you need to have a plan and adjust as you go.

I knew from a young age that I was smart. I knew I was really good at math. As a child, I dreamed of becoming a teacher once I got past the ballerina stage (that would never happen). I studied education in college and knew I would be a great teacher. The problem was that my parents wanted me to make enough money to be stable and support myself. My parents said no to teaching, so I switched to information technology. My dad also wanted me to get my master's degree. My mom truly thought I should work until I had children and then be an at-home mom like she was.

I knew I wanted to be my own boss someday and not have to be beholden to other bosses. I also wanted to make enough money to avoid being in debt. I wanted to have enough money saved for my children for college, to leave them money when I was gone, and to have a comfortable life. I wanted to buy whatever I wanted and not have to worry about how I would pay for it. I also knew I wanted to be a fun and loving grandmother someday. When I retired, I would do something to help other people. I had yet to learn when and how I would do all these things. I just knew if I had done all these things, I would have met my goals and been proud of myself.

Guess what? Nailed it! And now that I am retired from my original career, I'm anxious to give back and help others. I'm also now in a three-year doctoral program, and when I'm done, I plan to use this experience to help others succeed.

So, I am on my way to meeting all these goals. Have I done it all well? I believe so. I have succeeded through all the bumps in the road, all the mistakes along the way, all the second-guessing I've done, and all the stress, tears, and cheers.

My lessons learned are many. First and foremost, keep others from telling you what to do and how to do it. Had I listened to the naysayers, I would have quit my career as soon as my first daughter was born. Thank goodness, for my children's sake, I didn't do that. I was not the stay-at-home mom type of person. I was impatient, short-fused, and demanding. I was also funny; I played with them, taught them a lot, helped them with school, led the Girl Scout troop, and loved them with all my heart. I believe I am also a role model to them. They saw how a woman could succeed in her career and still be a loving mom, spouse, daughter, sister, and friend. I'm also a grandmother and continue to build memories with my grandchildren. I also enjoy spoiling them as much as possible.

Now, back to that health part. I am writing this section on a Monday. Today, I started my diet. No more carbs! It's time to walk ten thousand steps a day. Wish me luck.

Linda

I have spoken at conferences and similar venues. I have always been asked about work-life balance. My response has always been: There's no such thing. It's a fairy tale—a fantasy we entertain ourselves with while operating out of balance.

Work-life balance is the equilibrium between professional responsibilities and personal life, ensuring well-being and satisfaction. It involves managing time and energy to fulfill work and personal commitments, preventing burnout, reducing stress, and fostering healthy relationships. However, it's dynamic and requires regular reassessment. This equilibrium or harmony can be tenuous at best. Furthermore, we spend more time discussing balance than being *in* balance. Imagine that we are juggling multiple balls in the air—something drops, and we must chase the ball. Our lives are disequilibrium and teetering on the edge of chaos as we juggle and chase those balls.

Balls will certainly drop, and we will stumble and fall, yet how can we apply this linear concept of balance in our non-linear chaotic lives? How do we balance when simultaneously pulling our lives in many directions or dimensions?

You see, we aren't just juggling, for example, three balls in the air—one-third each, wife, daughter, CEO. We are juggling three whole people—a *whole* woman. We support ourselves non-linearly and follow the advice of the late marketing guru Clayton Christensen. Consider these questions:

- How can I be sure I will be successful <u>and</u> happy in my career?
- How can I be sure my relationships are an <u>enduring</u> source of happiness?
- How can I live a life of integrity?

Career Happiness

Career happiness is a personal journey that requires self-reflection, goal-setting, and informed choices. Essential tips include identifying values and passions, setting meaningful goals, finding a good fit, cultivating a positive mindset, nurturing positive relationships, and seeking work that aligns with one's purpose. It's important to regularly reassess career satisfaction and seek guidance from mentors or coaches. The thing to remember is that happiness is not a social construct. It is spiritual. Happiness does not come from the height of a linear career trajectory but from a multifaceted dimension based on meaning and purpose.

Enduring Relationships

Effective communication, mutual trust, emotional support, quality time together, flexibility, commitment, and continuous growth are essential for building and maintaining a happy, long-lasting relationship. These factors foster understanding, resolve conflicts, and strengthen emotional bonds. Providing emotional support, spending quality time together, being flexible, maintaining friendships, and having shared values contribute to a sense of security and stability. On the other hand, not all relationships should be enduring. I struggle with understanding that relationships can be for a reason, a season, or a lifetime.

A Life of Integrity

Living a life of integrity involves aligning actions, values, and beliefs and being honest, ethical, and consistent. To live with integrity, one must:

- Know your values.
- Be honest and transparent.
- Act ethically.
- Live up to commitments.
- Take responsibility for actions.
- Treat others with respect.
- Lead by example.
- Practice self-reflection.
- Be surrounded by like-minded individuals.
- Learn and grow continuously.

This journey requires self-awareness, conscious choices, and a commitment to personal growth. By staying true to values and aligning actions with them, one can cultivate a life of integrity and authenticity.

Finally, a life of balance does not exist in the fairy tale of spa appointments and cosmopolitans, but a state of being provides long-lasting rewards. This illusive balance is a *state of being*, not *doing*. However, we should always follow the advice of flight attendants and put on our oxygen masks first before helping others.

Jackie

Balance. What a great concept. So many things must be balanced in life—your health, career, relationships, happiness, responsibilities, finances, and mental health. The key is that at the core of this balance, it is and should be all about you and your needs. But often, you are put last behind others' needs.

Finding balance is such a great concept that it truthfully landed me in government employment years ago. I found myself in my mid-twenties as a government consultant supporting more than forty hours a week of client work. Then, in the evenings and weekends, I spent countless hours helping build the framework of the small business where I worked. After all, I had my master's in business administration and practical experience in leadership and human resources (HR) already, so I was ripe to help establish this small business' HR policies, procedures, compensation model, and more—all in my "free time." I was given the snazzy, high-profile title of principal, which carries weight in the government consulting world around the D.C. Beltway. With this title came the unspoken truth that I was expected to put in these extra hours and sweat equity to help advance the company. After all, wouldn't that only help me with job stability and career success in the long run? It all boiled down to my job being number one in my life, and all else would have to wait or suffer.

Fast-forward to 2010, and my work in consulting and helping build this small business was consuming my life. Work-life balance did not exist for me. I couldn't even tell you the definition of balance then! While the small business owner was sometimes generous, I worked many hours to line someone else's pockets. How charitable of me, right?

For a few years, my government client had been asking me to convert to become a federal employee, and I wasn't ready to take that leap—until now. My number one reason for jumping at this great opportunity was that I'd find work-life balance working for the government! I would finally only have to work a forty-hour work week and have time to go home to tend to life outside of work, and most importantly, take care of myself. Oh, how naïve I was!

The reality is that I've always struggled to find balance in my life. I'm self-motivated and love to take on big projects and multitask to an infinite degree. From the time I was a teenager, I would take on not just one full-time summer job but two. I would even pull back-to-back double shifts on weekends—ocean lifeguard by day, yacht club bartender by night. By the time school would roll around, I'd be exhausted, but I had a cushy bank account for my age. This carried on to college, where I was in honors classes and took on two majors. But I couldn't stop there, so I continued bartending and took on several shifts at the front desk of the Hotel Viking in Newport, Rhode Island. Fast-forward to my emergence into the "real world." I took on an expedited Master of Business Administration program at George Washington University while working full time. So, after my history of overexerting my time and energy, why did I think that suddenly I was going to find balance because of a job? The harsh truth is that finding balance has nothing to do with the job and everything to do with the person.

As a woman, I believe the societal pressures to have it all bear significant weight (pun intended) on us. In today's world, there is pressure to have an excellent job so we can be independent and not rely on a man to provide for us. We face extreme societal pressures to be naturally skinny and perfectly presented on the outside, no matter what is going on within. And, we're burdened with the gender-based expectations that we must settle down, have a family, and balance work with cooking, keeping a clean household, and living the perfect American dream. Now that social media is in the mix, these pressures are magnified to an extreme degree.

Well, my reality is *that* American dream isn't entirely *my* American dream. Luckily for me, the strong, independent woman that I am ensures I will not succumb to those societal "peer" pressures. I always knew I wanted to make something of myself and have an extensive career. I knew I would be an independent woman who didn't need a man to provide for me. For years, my dream was to be a corporate lawyer. However, my course changed when I was fortunate to be a White House intern in 2003. During my time in D.C., I was thriving. I loved being surrounded by motivated professionals and knew government work was where I belonged so that I could make a difference for our country. I grew up in a small, close-knit community in Rhode Island, where many people are born, raised, settle down, and never leave. I knew bigger things were in my blood. I certainly am not knocking my hometown, as generations of my family remain in Westerly today, and it still feels like home to me when I visit. It is a fantastic place to settle down and raise a family. It is simply that my American dream did not include raising a family, and I wasn't sure about my desire to get married then either.

So, within days of graduating from undergrad, I got in my car alone and drove to D.C. to find a job and an apartment. It was the beginning of the rest of my life. While D.C. has served me well career-wise, balancing my health has been a struggle. My weight has always been a challenge for me, with two major contributing factors: the stress of my career and genetics. I come from a long lineage of chubby Italians on my mother's side of the family. I recall my mom and grandma both going on many diets throughout my childhood but with limited success or results. We cook from the heart and find joy in feeding others—it is our love language. So, I succumbed to the fact that I, too, would be dieting and battling my weight for eternity. To me, brains and career success (literally) outweighed being perfectly skinny.

When I met Eric, my (now) husband, I wasn't looking for anything serious regarding a relationship. I was doing well in my career, but life was on an upward trajectory, and I certainly didn't need a relationship to derail my path. Soon enough, things got serious, and I found a permanent place in Eric's heart by feeding him. Several years of dating had passed, so Eric took me engagement ring shopping. Most women would be thrilled; I responded that we should sell my condo and buy a townhouse together to signify our commitment to each other instead of getting engaged. I was scared. How could I balance a marriage with a demanding career that lacked work life balance? My career has always been number one; how could I put someone else first? And where did taking care of myself fit into the picture?

It took years to realize that taking care of me comes first in the path to finding balance in life. I know that you cannot make someone else happy if you don't have true joy and happiness in your life. Therefore, my most extensive advice is to put yourself first because no one else in life will or can. And I mean no one. You must take action to manage your health, stress, and life. How can you bring your best self to your work, relationships, and family? By taking care of yourself first. It's such a simple concept that I hope many of you have already mastered it. Although it is a simple concept, it is one of the hardest I've been working to accomplish in life.

I still need help with this advice. While I realize I need to prioritize myself, putting it into practice is challenging. I've grown accustomed to the mentality of "I've got more work to do, so let me keep working." In recent years, I've found success in assuring myself that the work will be there for me tomorrow, and unless it is a matter of life or death (sometimes it is in my job), it can wait. As a leader, set the boundaries and lead by example. Your employees will take note and follow suit, so be cautious about the tone you're setting in the organization. Don't send emails late at night expecting people won't respond because they will. If you must get the thought out in a message, use the delayed delivery function in email to deliver it in the morning instead of after-hours at night. Your staff will thank you. And it will help their stress and well-being, too!

Let your team see you taking a vacation and unplugging from work. Trust that the team will get the job done without you and thank them for doing so when you return. Recently, at a work social hour, a couple of team members in my division specifically thanked me for taking vacations and modeling that it is essential to step away, recharge, and enjoy life. They expressed that having bosses in the past who didn't take vacations and who made them feel like they couldn't and shouldn't get away was brutal. We bond over talking about upcoming trips we have planned or time off to staycation and get things done at home. Such a novel concept relating to balance is what strengthens our connection as a team.

The bottom line is invest in taking care of yourself—whatever that means to you. Whether it is cooking, knitting, working out, being outside, or spending time with friends or family, find what brings you joy, stress relief, and inner peace, and do it! Prioritizing your well-being helps you find balance, sets a great example to those you lead, and strengthens all your relationships, including the most important one with yourself. Remember, if you don't take care of yourself, you cannot be your best self for others, both at home and in the workplace.

Tiffany

Balancing life as a woman today feels like juggling flaming torches while walking a tightrope—and doing it all with a smile. As a woman in my forties, I can tell you this act doesn't get easier with age. It just gets…different. With career progression, the evolving needs of family, and the elusive pursuit of self-care, the stakes only get higher.

As a C-suite executive, my professional life demands constant vigilance and dedication, but that's only one of the many hats I wear. I'm also a mother to a wonderful daughter, a wife, and a woman who sometimes wants a massage, a vacation without work emails, or even a quiet moment to herself.

I poured nearly everything into building my career for the first fourteen years of my daughter's life. I was a young mom, a wife, and a mid-level manager with something to prove. I worked around the clock, studying and climbing the ladder. If you can relate, you know what I mean when I say I was present but not present.

I brought my laptop everywhere—vacations, track practices, you name it. When I wasn't typing, I was on my phone: taking calls, answering emails, or working on deliverables. I was habitually late to daycare pickups, concerts, and parties. My daughter eventually caught on. "Mom, I know you'll be late," she would say, "but try to be on time."

Then, during her freshman year of high school, she hit me with a wake-up call. "You've got less than four years before I'm out of the house," she reminded me. And just like that, the countdown began: 893 days. Then, 654 days. Then 345. You get the idea.

It was then that I realized I had to do better—not just for her but also for myself. I couldn't undo the years of late arrivals and distracted evenings, but I could show her what it meant to be fully present.

Fast-forward to today: She's a rising junior in college, thriving in ways that make me endlessly proud. Her first year wasn't easy; she was homesick a lot and I missed her terribly. There were days when I'd drive two hours just to have lunch with her, check on her well-being, and remind her that home was always within reach. And when I wasn't in person, I was there on the phone—listening as she vented about professors, roommate drama, or breathing quietly on the other end of the line because she needed me to.

Of course, being a mother isn't my only role. I'm also a wife, working to be present for my husband amid corporate strategies and board meetings. And then there's me—the woman who needs self-care, time for Pilates sessions, doctor's visits, and moments of peace.

People often suggest I let something go, but each role I carry is a thread in the fabric of who I am. They all matter—to me and to the life I'm building.

Yet, as women, we constantly navigate a narrative that expects us to do it all—this story of strength and endurance glosses over our silent struggles to maintain equilibrium.

Yes, men face challenges balancing work, family, and personal life, but let's be honest: The playing field is rarely equal. Many male colleagues in professional settings have wives who traditionally manage the home, the meals, and the children. This dynamic often creates unspoken pressures on women to excel both at work and at home.

And then there are the double standards. A man can spend every night networking, attending conferences, and advancing his career without a second thought, but when a woman does the same, she risks being labeled as neglectful, a "bad mom" or a "distant wife."

These biases don't just hold women back; they perpetuate the idea that our worth is tied to traditional gender roles. It's a weight we carry; too often, it's invisible to those around us.

In my forties, I'm finally learning to let go of some of these pressures. These days, I log off at five or six p.m., no longer interrupting family dinners for calls or burning the midnight oil. I sit at the table—no phone in sight—and engage in real conversations with my family.

I take walks in the middle of the day. I meditate, even if just for five minutes, to center myself. These small acts of self-care remind me that balance isn't something you find; it's something you create.

For the women reading this, I want you to know that it's okay to prioritize yourself. Here's what I've learned along the way:

Prioritize self-care. Your physical, mental, and emotional well-being are essential. Make time for exercise, relaxation, and the things that bring you joy.

Set boundaries. Learn to say no without guilt. Protect your time and energy by only taking on what you can handle.

Invest in relationships. Be present with the people you love. Put away your phone, turn off notifications, and give them your full attention. Quality time builds stronger connections and shows your loved ones they matter.

Advance Your career. Pursue your goals passionately and firmly, but don't let society's expectations dictate your choices.

Balancing life as a woman isn't about perfection—it's about presence. It's about showing up for yourself, your family, and your dreams in meaningful ways. This journey isn't easy, but it's worth it. Trust in your abilities, honor your values and embrace every step with resilience and grace.

Chapter 7:
The Impostor Syndrome

Even the most accomplished of us grapple with feelings of self-doubt and inadequacy. In this chapter, we delve into the pervasive nature of impostor syndrome and its impact on our confidence. We share how we silence that inner critic, own our accomplishments, and step boldly into our power.

Helene

I must admit that I have never heard of the term *impostor syndrome*, so I Googled it. It is a behavioral health phenomenon described as self-doubt of intellect, skills, or accomplishments among high-achieving individuals. You experience that uncomfortable feeling when you think you're unqualified and incompetent. You might look around and assume everyone except you knows what they're doing. And if you achieve something good, you'll chalk your accomplishment up to "good luck."

When I think of this syndrome, the word *self-esteem* comes to mind. How often does someone say something positive to you, and your initial internal reaction is, *Who, me?* Then, externally, you might look beside or behind you, wondering if they meant to compliment someone else. How many people honestly say they have not experienced this at some point? I certainly have in the past and occasionally do so even now. Throughout my career, I've experienced self-doubt, fear of failure, second-guessing, and the concern of standing out as someone who doesn't get it. When I became a leader, the feelings did not go away, but I learned how to hide them. I believed that if I told my team that I did not know something, they would lose respect for me or at least not want to follow my direction. Think of a military leader who wants to charge the enemy. If they said, "Troops, let's do this attack, but first, does anyone know where, when, and how because I don't," would the troops have any confidence in their leader? I doubt it. However, a big difference between military and business leaders is life and death. If a business leader said, "I want to go after this contract. Still, I don't have the strategy down pat," instead of not following this leader, the team would most likely feel empowered. The team supporting this leader would be able to provide input in their areas of expertise, and the sales strategy would be more robust. This is one of the most important lessons I learned early in my leadership roles. A true leader should surround themselves with people more intelligent than themselves. If a leader is the most knowledgeable person on the team, there's no one they can depend on for help. However, it is a tricky situation. At what point will the team lose faith in the leader, and how much should the leader show their weakness and lack of personal confidence?

As female leaders in what is still considered a male-dominated field, we are already at a disadvantage. We may need help with our leadership style (assertive versus aggressive, intuitive versus logical). Some of us took time off to raise children or to care for our elders. Some are starting a family, and there is uncertainty about how long they will take off for maternity leave or whether they will decide to stay at home. Some of us might be too young, too pretty, too sexy, too shy, or too meek. Many hurdles with gender equity impact how we are perceived as a leader. So much of our time is spent overcoming the perception of being a "female boss." Then there are the behavioral issues. Women are accused of being catty, manipulative, pushy, competitive, and emotionally weak. To top it all off, some of these accusations are true. I've always said that we women can sometimes be our own worst enemy. I reflect on some female managers I have had and have seen some of these behaviors. I've also seen the same in male managers, but somehow, they've learned to mask it better.

Now, back to the subjects of self-esteem and confidence. I had a huge confidence issue in my career. I knew I was smart. I knew I was intuitive. I knew I could always see the big picture. I also knew I had little patience with people who couldn't keep up with me and my plans. Not only that, but I knew that I was always thin-skinned and could easily be hurt. So, I shaped my leadership style to avoid failure, hide my insecurities, and protect myself from hurt. The problem was I needed to remember to protect others.

One day, a colleague approached me and said, "People are uncomfortable on your team because you are too direct, and they need to be on guard constantly. Maybe you should turn it down a notch." My reaction was, "I'm not here to be liked. I'm here to win business." At that point, he shrugged and walked away. Years later, I now know what he meant. He meant if you're not here to be liked and don't care what people think, you will reap what you sow. You may win the deal, but people will avoid you as their leader next time. I knew I wasn't liked and acted like I didn't care, but I cared a lot. I wanted to be liked. I wanted people to be on my team. I couldn't figure out how to "dial it back." I was confident in leading a team to win the deal. Still, I needed to be more confident in being accepted as a leader. And when we did win, and the accolades were given, I was one to say that it took a team to win, but the team did not always believe my words.

Fast forward to now. I have figured out a few things in the last few years. First, we don't change our core personality traits as we age. I still need to gain more patience with people and keep up with my pace in completing tasks and making decisions. I make decisions fast, sometimes too fast. The good side is that I am agile and can adapt to any situation. I can also adjust my communication style and body language to relate to most audiences. There's a downside, and it's costly. I make snap decisions, which can be very reckless and expensive in time and money. Many times, I have buyer's remorse.

Also, I cancel plans because I tend to second guess myself (an effect of impostor syndrome). However, what can change with time is the ability to think of how your behavior affects others. I call this the kinder and gentler Helene. As I used to say, I'm not here to be liked; I do care how others perceive me. Since I'm at the age where I'm focused on much more than my career and family, I can now slow down things and think of how what I say and do affects others. I now know that we all have our demons. Everyone suffers in some way from impostor syndrome, and it's our responsibility to help others have easier and happier lives. I'm also less insecure. I am proud of myself. I am a loving mother, grandmother, wife, sister, and friend. I've done well in my career and am still working on it. I am intelligent, funny, and generous, and I continue to work on me, for me and for those I care about. I am a work in progress, and that's okay with me.

I advise readers to get to know what you know and don't know. Surround yourself with people who know more about what you don't know as much about. Know how others perceive you and decide how you want to be regarded—someone once told me to write what I want others to say at my funeral and then work to become that person. And mostly, love yourself. Be your own advocate. Be proud of you! Lastly, don't worry—everyone around you is going through the same thing. We all second guess ourselves, sometimes feel insecure, and can doubt ourselves. Spend time helping others feel better about themselves, and you will also benefit from this. Mentor those who are open to learning from you; for those who are not, leave the door open if they ever need your advice. Be good to others and be good to yourself.

Linda

One of the most crippling inhibitors to our achievements will be the self-induced anxiety known as *fear of success*. Psychologist Abraham Maslow called this fear the *Jonah Complex*. The name comes from the biblical prophet Jonah, who God called to do great things for the people of Nineveh. Jonah, believing that the problems of Nineveh were too significant for him to resolve, sought to escape God by boat. God thwarted his efforts by sending a storm of such divine intensity that Jonah's shipmates decided to toss him overboard. He was immediately swallowed by a great fish and was trapped in its belly for three days. After the fish vomited him up, Jonah learned his lesson and went to Nineveh to achieve his destined greatness.

Maslow describes this as "fear of one's greatness," "evasion of one's destiny," or "running away from one's own best talents." We are afraid of achieving the most incredible possibilities, under the most extraordinary courage, in our most perfect moments. As overachieving women, we often measure ourselves with an unrealistic measuring stick. We fear we will always fall short no matter how much we have achieved. That is fear of failure.

Here are three thoughts:

You can run, but you can't hide. Jonah had talents that he ran away from. I tried to run, but it didn't work. You may try that, too. It won't work. I have a talent for teaching, but I gave it up to make more money. When I first founded Muse Technologies, Inc., I ignored the calling of teaching, coaching, and mentoring. For that reason, I have been in the belly of the beast for a decade. Here I am. Four teaching opportunities have crossed my path several decades later. The time has now come for the hiding to stop.

You must have faith. In the movie *Raiders of the Lost Ark*, our protagonist, the main character, Indiana Jones, must step out of faith. He must step into what appears to be a dark abyss with no passageway in front of him. He is given a riddle telling him to step out on faith to obtain one of his sought artifacts. When he takes a step forward, a path materializes. We often need to be bold about taking that first step. Because of this fear, we need courage. With courage, fear is just the beginning of your path to greatness.

Courage comes from the heart. The word *courage* has its roots in the Old French language, meaning "heart" or "innermost feelings." It is derived from the Latin word *coraticum* and the Proto-Indo-European root *kerd-*. The connection between heart and courage is evident in various languages and cultures, symbolizing the ability to face and overcome challenges. Another way to understand this connection between heart and courage is through the word *passion*. I finished a full-time Ph.D. program while running a company because I am passionate about organizational leadership *and* my company, Muse. As a Baptist preacher once told me, passion gives you the means to endure suffering.

To those earlier in their career, my advice is not to wait to be puked up by a great fish but to recognize the greatness you've been called to TODAY. Now that you have some clues about overcoming your performance anxieties, how can you not aspire to be great? What are your most incredible possibilities? We _can_ achieve and maintain business success. We _can_ achieve and maintain harmonious family relationships. We are good enough, we deserve it, and who cares who is watching? And we will do this first by heeding your calling, having faith, and welcoming fear as the harbinger of courage.

Jackie

Writing this chapter, I had to look up the definition of *impostor syndrome* to ensure I had it right. I located many definitions and even lengthy articles that included several different types of impostor syndrome. Quite overwhelming, if you ask me! So, for purposes of this chapter, I'm sticking to the definition that resonated the most with me from good, old, reliable *Merriam-Webster*. Impostor syndrome is "a psychological condition characterized by persistent doubt concerning one's abilities or accomplishments and the fear of being exposed as a fraud despite evidence of one's ongoing success."

Sitting with that definition, I can feel it. As I've grown in my career and am considering taking that next step, I've always questioned whether I fit every role qualification. I have held back from taking chances, jumping at opportunities, and exploring the unknown in a new position or organization because of self-doubt. Impostor syndrome has kept me in the very same place for many years now. Am I comfortable? Yes. Do I know what I'm doing and continue to grow my organization? Yes. Do I see others as not qualified to get prominent positions and promotions? Yes. Do I put myself out there and apply for those big jobs or entertain huge roles? No. Why not, you may ask? Well, impostor syndrome, that's why!

Several years ago, I was at a retirement celebration for a colleague who mentioned that his only regret in his career was staying somewhere too long and not seeking the next opportunity. He didn't mean it in the sense that he overstayed his welcome or didn't continue achieving great things; he meant it in the sense of getting comfortable and letting that comfort keep him where he was instead of moving on to the next position that would challenge him. Thinking about what he was saying way back then resonates now as I'm thinking about what's next. Let's face it: I've grown and been comfortable for too long. But something inside is holding me back—the fear of inadequacy.

I love challenges—I embrace them and cannot back down from something because it is hard. However, it seems I've hit a plateau in my professional life, where I've settled on being comfortable. I'm the first to critique and say, "How the hell did so and so" get *that* job?" But I'm also the one who felt I couldn't fit the bill, so I didn't apply or express interest. The reality is I'll never get *that* job if I don't apply or express that I'm interested. It is like I've got these huge weights on my shoulders holding me back and a voice telling me I'm not qualified or able to do it.

I've become someone heavily relied upon on our team at work. My bosses tell me they can always count on me to take on a challenge and deliver—whether or not it is in my lane or area of expertise. My colleagues frequently ask me to help lead joint projects with them because they can rely on my technical and leadership skills. So, rationalizing why I feel inadequate for the next big thing when I'm a proven entity in my organization is hard to swallow. It's like I'm paralyzed by considering what is next.

So, how do I get over this? Honestly, I'm not sure. But the good news is that I know I do not need to navigate it alone! I have found some exceptional mentors who are my biggest cheerleaders. Recently, a higher-level executive position opened outside my current office, and I joked about putting my name in it. My rationale to my mentors was that I could easily do that job in my sleep. Instead of encouraging me to go ahead and apply, they told me this was not the right opportunity for me. Then, they used my own words against me. The fact that I said I could easily do this job in my sleep was the reason they said it was not for me. I wouldn't be pushing myself and undertaking a challenge—it would be more of the same cruise control without really growing professionally. I realize I need to grow comfortable with getting uncomfortable in a role to grow professionally. If I don't challenge myself, how will I grow? Skills need to be exercised; therefore, pushing myself into roles that enable me to continue to grow is an essential piece of my next chapter.

So, what advice applies when I'm still working through this challenge myself? First and foremost, if you don't apply for the position, someone else will. Someone possibly less qualified than you will get it. Instead of doubting your value and capabilities, put yourself out there because you cannot get that job if you don't apply. Second, if you feel comfortable where you are, consider seeking a mentor's advice on where and what to do next. I'm not advocating for you to prematurely job jump. I'm advocating for you to perform your work to the best of your ability, and once you have demonstrated measurable successes and accomplishments, consider what is and should be next professionally. Your résumé will not write itself. Approach each position as one where you can succinctly write what you accomplished with tangible outcomes and determine when you're done growing in that role. If you've met a path where, for years, the line in your résumé would read "kept the lights on and cruise control active," it's time to move on.

Finally, when you hear incredible stories of other leaders and women who have made it big, don't think, *Wow, I could never do that*. Instead, think, *I'm going to get there someday, too*. It's all about not letting impostor syndrome prevent us from greatness and stifle our professional journey. As my parents always said, you can be anything you want if you put your mind to it!

Tiffany

Picture this: You're climbing the career ladder in your twenties or thirties, confident in your abilities one moment and then gripped by a sinking feeling the next. That relentless tug-of-war with impostor syndrome sneaks in, whispering, *"Are you sure you're good enough?"* That was me when I stepped into my first management role. It was a crossroads moment that left me wrestling with questions of identity, capability, and belonging.

In the early 2000s, the specter of affirmative action loomed large in corporate circles. It planted doubt in my mind, making me wonder whether my promotion reflected my merit or simply a box checked for diversity. Even with intelligence and dedication on my side, that nagging whisper—*You're not supposed to be here*—echoed in my thoughts.

I did everything I could to fit in. Promoted to leadership, I mirrored the fashion sense of my predecessors, primarily white women. My wardrobe became a predictable palette of blues, browns, blacks, and grays—safe, unobtrusive, and forgettable. Fear tethered me to the norms, suppressing any desire to step outside the lines or, heaven forbid, *stand out*.

Then, in 2006, I got thrown into the deep end—building a call center from the ground up. I had no playbook, just grit, a knack for hiring good people, and perhaps too much bravado. Deep down, I felt entirely out of my depth, but I kept showing up, figuring it out as I went, and learning to tread water in uncharted territory.

By 2008, I'd transitioned into a government role—an entirely new ballgame. Terms like *business development, profit margins*, and *contracts* were thrown around like confetti, and I had no idea what they meant. EBITDA (Earnings Before Interest, Taxes, Depreciation, and Amortization) and M&A (Mergers and Acquisitions)? They may as well have been hieroglyphs. I spent countless late nights burning the midnight oil, trying to decode these new rules and climb this seemingly insurmountable mountain.

The higher I climbed, the louder that whisper of self-doubt became. I constantly worried my colleagues would see through me like I was a fraud. Asking questions felt risky—what if they thought I wasn't competent enough or qualified? I had to project confidence, even when I was unsure.

And I'm not alone in this. Women seem to grapple with impostor syndrome on a different level, juggling professional challenges while navigating societal expectations and gender norms. Consider spaces like golf courses—long seen as arenas for networking and deal-making. For women, they can feel more like battlegrounds for self-doubt as we try to navigate these traditionally male-dominated spaces.

While I still wrestle with moments of self-doubt in my current role, I no longer feel the pressure to conform. There's often an unspoken expectation that compliance and deference are rewarded, while disagreement can quickly sideline you. Navigating this dynamic requires striking a delicate balance between speaking up and maintaining your place at the table.

But here's the thing—I'm no longer worried about keeping my seat at the table. I know I've earned it, and if others aren't comfortable with my presence, that's their issue, not mine. The reality is, I'm not going anywhere. I bring value to the table and am here to contribute, not blend in.

If I could go back in time, I'd give my younger self one piece of advice: Stop chasing perfection. Perfection is a mirage. It's unattainable, and the pursuit of it only holds you back. I spent too many years worrying about how I measured up instead of focusing on learning and building my strengths.

Winning the Battle with Impostor Syndrome

So, how do you overcome that sneaky voice that tells you you're not enough? Here are some strategies that worked for me—and maybe they'll work for you too:

Recognize doubt is normal. You're not crazy, and you're not alone. Many high achievers wrestle with self-doubt. Even the people you admire most have likely questioned themselves at some point.

Call out negative thoughts. That voice in your head telling you you're a fraud, it's lying. Challenge it. Write down those thoughts and counter them with facts about your abilities and achievements.

Keep a brag folder. Save emails, notes, or anything that acknowledges your contributions and successes. When self-doubt creeps in, take a moment to flip through it. It's a powerful reality check.

Set achievable goals. Don't try to conquer the world in one day. Break down big goals into smaller, manageable steps. Celebrate every win along the way—it all adds up.

Find a mentor. A mentor who's been in your shoes can be a game changer. They can offer guidance, share their experiences, and remind you that you can succeed.

Focus on learning, not perfection. Nobody knows everything. The most successful people are lifelong learners. Every question you ask and every mistake you make are opportunities to grow.

Reflect on your strengths. Take time to think about what you're good at and what brings you joy. Knowing your strengths is a huge confidence booster.

The truth is impostor syndrome isn't a reflection of your inadequacy; it's a symptom of a society that still struggles with inclusivity and equity. Women face double standards, unspoken expectations, and cultural norms that make us question our worth in ways men rarely experience.

But here's the empowering part: Once you recognize those whispers of doubt for what they are, you can start to silence them. Advocate for yourself. Speak up for your female colleagues. Celebrate your wins, no matter how small they seem.

And remember this: You are not here by accident. You've earned your seat at the table, your place in the room, and the right to take up space. So, own it. Speak with confidence, even when you feel unsure. Show up authentically, even when the world feels unkind.

The only thing more powerful than self-doubt is the determination to overcome it.

Chapter 8:
Ageism

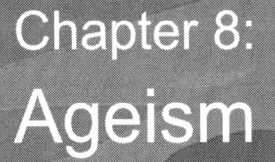

As we grow older, we often face biases that challenge our relevance and value in the workplace. This chapter sheds light on the realities of ageism and how we overcome stereotypes to leverage our experience as a strength. Together, we explore how wisdom and adaptability pave the way for continued success and influence.

Helene

Ageism. No Googling needed. I've got my definition. It is the act of starting as the youngest in the company; before you know it, you're one of the oldest, and Medicare is now on the horizon. This is a natural part of a career; understanding it can help alleviate anxiety about workplace aging.

This chapter is not meant to be depressing. It's a heads-up and some advice. Everyone, hopefully, will grow old. It's okay. It's better than the alternative! It's not how you will deal with it; it's more about having and executing a plan. By understanding the career lifecycle and planning for changes, you can navigate the aging process in the workplace with confidence and control.

At the time of publishing this book, I am sixty-five years old. How on earth did this happen? Yesterday, I was the new kid on the block. Let's face it: who remembers everything that happened between twenty-one and sixty-five? I can barely remember what I had for dinner last night. That's why résumés were invented. Sure, they help hire managers, but they are handy for people who need to fill out applications. It's hard to remember all the places most of us have worked over a lifetime.

Let's review the lifecycle of a career: We start right after graduation from school (high school or college). Your first job, let's face it, you are in a fog. You're trying to figure out how to order supplies, where to go for lunch, what the company you work for does, and what your roles and responsibilities are. A year goes by, and you finally know where you work and what you do. The company you work for now knows whether you are someone they want to keep around or whether they should help you with career résumé tips. Usually, by then, you also start to find out how much money you make versus your friends versus your coworkers. That's when you decide whether you want to stay or go. Either way, year two comes about, and you start to realize you're still super young, and there's going to be people who join the company who are younger than you, and you can help them get through the fog.

Fast forward to years two through ten. You are still young. Your current company has you figured out. They know whether you're a keeper who will be steady and continue to deliver, whether you're a future superstar, which is sometimes referred to as a high-potential worker, or whether, once again, they may offer to help you update your résumé. You may also be focused on establishing a family.

From years eleven to thirty, you are now in the thick of your career. You have a 401(k) fund established that your company is hopefully contributing to. If you have children, hopefully, you have established a college fund. You have a mortgage and car payment(s). Your parents are heading toward retirement. You have three weeks' vacation. Your salary is steadily increasing, and your bonuses are cool. You use every sick day you are given for all the crud your kids bring home from daycare or school. You are steadily moving up the career path. Companies are investing in you by sending you to training classes and conferences. You're in your thirties and forties. You know what you are good at and what you are not. And you most likely are coasting along with maybe five-year goals but not ten. This is the best time for your career—you are on fire.

Now you are fifty! How on earth did this happen? Your salary is maxed out. Your 401(k) is not where you thought it would be because you did not max out on your withholding since you needed money for your kid's college, to fix up the house, vacations, and, of course, the designer bags and cool clothes that you still fit into but may be getting a bit tight. You must use some of your three-to-four weeks accrued vacations to care for your aging parents or your spouse's knee replacement. And then there's work. You are no longer the youngest. You're not even the coolest. You are now middle-aged, and your company knows it. Now you feel the reality. You make a lot of money and may not be at this company in ten years.

As many people in their fifties are hiring managers, they hear human resources say (not in public), "When looking for employees, look for people that make less than you do and are younger than you." You start to realize that many companies do the math. They can hire two people for one middle-aged person; even if they need to be more adept, they can learn. Who is the teacher? The fifty-year-old. There's another idea that senior leaders come up with. Let's have the fifty-plus-year-olds document how they do their job, and then not only can they teach the young'uns, but now we have everything documented. Then, we can help them with their résumé since we have everything we need.

And then you are sixty-plus. You may have lost a parent or both. You are not only not young, but you are now getting ten percent off on Tuesdays at your favorite breakfast chain.

You now know how much money is in your 401(k) and how many years it will last you after retirement. You also know how much Social Security you will get. You discover that your company's health plan is much better than Medicare. You may be considering moving to warmer climates and struggling with being a long-distance grandmother. You also realize that the chances of finding a new job or staying relevant in your current job could be better. And you need every sick day available cause your body is going downhill.

Wow, this is depressing, but is it? Because in our sixties, we women have many good things going on. Our kids are out of college, making money, and don't need our money. Many of our children have also found their soul mates and started independent lives. We still look and feel pretty good. We don't have to dye our hair or wear makeup or business suits. We are postmenopausal. We can afford some of the designer things we always wanted. We can travel, play games, enjoy hobbies, and hang out with friends. We may have grandchildren now and can send them home when they get cranky or sick. We have girlfriends and guy friends, and if we are married, it's probably because we chose a spouse to grow old with us. We also know ourselves so much better and have accepted who we are. Finally, we can decide how to spend the final third of our life. Do we want to work full- or part-time in our current field? Do we want to change careers? Do we want to go back to school? Do we want to volunteer? Do we want to travel? Do we want to play? And if more than one, what combination of these choices is best for us?

Now for advice. First, don't think that life will be different for you. Yes, you may stay with the same company for a long time. You may keep moving up the ladder and work until your seventies or longer. You may retire in your forties or fifties. Regardless, we all start young and age. My one piece of advice is to have a plan. Plan out where you see yourself fresh out of school, where you see yourself as you grow your family, where you see yourself in the prime of your career, where you see yourself in your fifties (hot flashes and all), and what your retirement will look like. The plan will fluctuate, but overall, set goals and stay focused on those milestones.

I have a plan. It changed a bit, but I remained focused. I started wanting to be a teacher but followed the money (and my parents' advice). I became a technical person who utilized math and logic. I moved into management in my mid-thirties. I went into strategic sales in my forties. I had a blip in the plan as I got breast cancer in my fifties and had to readjust. I went through my fifties, becoming overpriced and obsolete to companies, so I started my own company, which took off.

I sold my company in my early sixties. My husband and I moved to Florida to live on a golf course. I then went back to school to get my doctorate. Then, we bought a home in Virginia to live in Florida in the winter and be close to our family in the hotter months. Did I hit bumps along the road and adjust? Absolutely! But I had a plan and adjusted as I went. I planned to raise exceptional children, get my master's degree, excel in my career, mentor others, have grandchildren, own my own company, sell it, get my doctorate, and help others handle their career blips. All the while, I have amazing friends, a loving spouse, and enough money to live a comfortable lifestyle. I nailed it!

Linda

See? I snuck in a chapter on my hair. So, let's dive into the enchanting world of Black women and their marvelous hair! Prepare to be whisked away on a magical journey filled with tales of rich history, cultural significance, and the whimsical challenges that come with it. How delightful it is to recognize the profound connection between hair and cultural heritage! You see, darling, hairstyles have this enchanting ability to express one's personal style and deep-rooted connection to the marvelous African traditions. Oh, how we adore the boundless versatility and enchanting creativity of styling Black hair! From the mesmerizing array of natural styles to the magical world of protective techniques, we can't help but celebrate the sheer beauty and wonder that unfolds before our eyes. Behold the enchanting dialogue that acknowledges the wondrous and ever-so-significant historical and sociopolitical implications! For you see, dear reader, Black women have been burdened with the weighty expectations of conforming to those Eurocentric beauty standards. Oh, the trials and tribulations they have endured!

So, what does this have to do with ageism?

You see, I was always the youngest in my profession. I worked at the Department of Commerce as a student assistant cartographer at seventeen. I was the youngest working as a Weapons Systems Management Development Program mathematician. I was the youngest career senior executive at the Department of Energy. In these "youngest" positions, I learned how to find my voice—I knew what I wanted and how I would do it. I was brave due to a lifetime of being "the only one" or "the youngest." So, there were advantages to being the youngest…until you're not.

I woke up one day with gray hair—nothing a bottle of temporary rinse couldn't handle. *Whew!* My hair was young again. I retired from the government and started a government contracting company. Suddenly, I was a useless old bag—sans gray hair.

However, I read somewhere that people were happiest when they found out they didn't have long to live. They then lived the last days of their lives to the fullest, stopping to smell the roses and spending time with those they loved.

I decided to stop coloring my hair and to enjoy the last days of my life—whether it is days, weeks, months, years, or decades. I was the oldest in my PhD program and finished the race to the completed dissertation faster than any of those youngbloods in my program. I look at my gray hair every morning and think *I don't have long to live, so I had better make this day count.* As I enter the life phase where I am taking care of my elders (84-year-old mother and 101-year-old grandfather), I only hope that I can make their days happy.

Yes, ageism is a real thing. It depends on your perspective—and also on your hair.

Jackie

Age is just a number. Some people have great genetics and look much more youthful than their age; others aren't so lucky. It is a natural tendency for people to consider someone too young or too old for something. In my current (middle) age, I struggle with being referred to as "ma'am" and am longing to be called "miss" once again. I thought that I'd be at a ripe place where being looked at as too young to accomplish something would no longer apply, but sad to say, it isn't true.

When I became a federal government employee in 2010, I worked in the organization for three years alongside the federal employees as a consultant. I helped establish the organizational structure and concept of operations. I laid the foundation for what it was with a group of fellow consultants and a couple of capable government employees. The rest of the government employees were the product of promotion up and out. The federal pay and promotion system is fundamentally broken, and I could write an entire book on it but that's not what this chapter is about! The bottom line is that when you have an underperforming employee, and they are eligible for promotion to a higher pay grade outside of the organization, you are enticed to give them a stellar review so that they leave and become someone else's problem. This practice, you see, is easier than holding the employee accountable for performing, documenting at length the performance issues, and going through the vicious cycle of attempting to either get someone to perform or to remove them. Plus, there's a lot of risk with the latter pathway. So, the path of least resistance is usually chosen. Like my organization, you get stuck with underperforming employees with limited capability capped out in pay grade at the GS-15 level, unable to go elsewhere because no one wants them, and they can't advance any further.

When my government boss was bringing me on board, he was able to justify bringing me in at the top grade of GS-15 on the pay scale. I had proven my capabilities for three years and consistently outperformed many of his existing federal employees. I was a principal at a consulting firm, and my salary was already at that level, so it was appropriate from a skill and capability standpoint and a compensation perspective. In addition, I ran circles around some of the federal employees, so how could he not bring me in at their level? Unfortunately, my government boss hated the administrative paperwork required in the hiring process and leveraged one of my soon-to-be colleagues to oversee the process. Her role overseeing my hiring action gave her access to my job offer and terms. She soon learned I was being brought onto the team at the same pay grade. She was appalled and let me know. I was only twenty-eight years old, and she had worked just as long in her career to reach the same grade level, and here I was, entering the government.

After my onboarding transition, my colleague mentioned my grade level in a conversation one day. She looked at me and said, "I was shocked when processing your paperwork that you were brought in at a GS-15. It took me nearly thirty years to get my GS-15, and here you are, just being handed it at such a young age." Her comment hurt. Didn't she see that after three years working alongside her, I was worthy of being brought in at this level, regardless of my age? What does age have to do with capability?

I wish I could share that this was the last time I was subjected to comments about my age and career accomplishments, but it wasn't. I soon learned that within the government, some people wear their general schedule grade level or senior executive service status on their sleeve. It's a code of valor that has been earned, and with its honor came the years of agony and hard work of edging up the government's general schedule ladder system. These grade designations are not only an indicator of pay but are widely used to determine where you are in your career.

If you've had the pleasure of being within the D.C. bubble for any time professionally, you know that folks lead conversations with the questions of "What do you do?" and "Who do you work for?" I must admit it, after being here for twenty years, I, too, do this. To me, it's the same as dogs who sniff each other's butts to get to know each other. D.C. is a small city, so these questions I've learned over the years are about making connections and understanding who knows who to help facilitate connections. I find them harmless, while others, especially outsiders, may find them pretentious and off-putting. To each their own. Even today, people either assume I'm at a much lower level than I am or are surprised when I tell them I've been a government executive for several years.

The truth is that I've never chased a grade level or position and never felt like my age should constrain me. I've focused on accomplishing the work at hand and delivering outcomes. This approach has served me well, so I climbed the government ladder and became an executive fairly early in life if I'm benchmarking my path against others. I met this career milestone surrounded by two groups: my biggest cheerleaders, who were authentically happy for my success and genuinely knew that I deserved the position, and those who looked at me simply by my age and thought I was too young for this level.

I often hear of people focusing on becoming a member of the Senior Executive Service (SES) instead of focusing on what they can show that demonstrates accomplishments to qualify for an SES. The latter piece is important; some people will never figure that out even when they've hit whatever magical age they believe is right for an SES. In general, symbolic career doorways do not open on their own. And if you think they do, it's likely because someone has recognized competence, capability, and quality therefore, they've held the door open for you based on your merits. To me, age isn't part of the equation.

I recently attended an event at work, and several young (and impressive) staffers from Capitol Hill were there. My colleague and I, who are about the same age and joined the senior executive service around the same time, joked about how we used to be the fresh-faced, youthful "kids" whom everyone talked about having a high position for our age. We laughed about how we're now middle-aged but still face comments from others. Observing those young staffers never triggered us to think they shouldn't be at such an event because they're so young. We didn't question whether they even had the proper knowledge or experience. Our experiences with ageism have led us to appreciate the next generation coming up through the ranks while acknowledging the hard truth that we're now in our middle-aged prime.

The adage stands true: Don't judge a book by its cover. A person's age is not indicative of experience, knowledge, capability, or worthiness of a position. Give older and younger people a chance to demonstrate capability before you judge it. Appreciate that if you put those judgments aside, you can focus your energy on what you can learn from each person, regardless of age. Additionally, never let age hold you back or be an indicator of where you should be in life or your career. Focus your energy on accomplishments in your career journey. Think about what the storyline and narrative would be on your résumé. What are the outcomes and impact delivered as a result of your accomplishments? Avoid at all costs benchmarking where you are career-wise to expectations tied to age, and certainly avoid holding yourself back because of age. Go for it if you qualify and have the capabilities!

Tiffany

Every age has its unique beauty, wisdom, and strength—at least, that's what people say to make getting older feel less daunting. But let's be honest: Society now loves to remind us of subtly and blatantly where it thinks we belong based on how many candles are on our last birthday cake. Ageism is that unseen force, a ghost in the machine, quietly shaping how others perceive us and, sometimes, how we perceive ourselves.

I wish I'd figured all of this out sooner. It took me more than forty years to realize that every phase of life is a new chapter, a mix of fears, self-doubts, triumphs, and lessons that only time can give. Now that I'm in what some might call the "peak of enjoyment" stage of life, I'm also preparing for the downside—whatever that means. Yet, as I reflect on the journey, one truth stands out: Each age carries its magic, even if society often tries to dull its shine.

My corporate journey began in my twenties when I had the energy of youth but none of the insider knowledge. I didn't come from a family steeped in corporate traditions. There were no cheat codes handed down to me for navigating the office maze. Instead, I stumbled through, learning the hard way.

Dress codes, the appropriate amount of jewelry, the fine line between professional and personal makeup—it was a minefield. Like most young professionals, I wanted to push boundaries, but not enough to lose my job. Case in point: I got a tongue piercing in college. Six months into my first job at a prestigious bank, I was promoted to lead and coached a team of twelve to fifteen technicians. During one session, I couldn't help but notice a colleague staring at my tongue ring the entire time. The look in her eyes screamed, *"Is this girl serious?"* That night, I reluctantly retired the tongue ring. I wanted to stand out professionally, not as the manager with an accessory that jingled during meetings.

In those early years, I also hid my actual age. It wasn't deceitful—it was strategic. I figured no one would take a young twenty-something seriously in a leadership role, so I sprinkled on a few extra professional years. *Maybe*, I thought, *if they think I'm twenty-eight instead of twenty-two, they'll respect me more.*

Looking back, I wish I'd embraced my youth instead of trying to fit into a corporate mold that didn't reflect my identity. I wanted so badly to belong to a world dominated by older, predominantly white professionals. Somewhere along the way, I forgot the power of being unapologetically authentic.

The Gift of Perspective

Fast-forward twenty years. Today, I'm undeniably older (let's just say wiser), and I sometimes long for the days when I was the young upstart making waves in the room. But there's a beauty to this stage of life, too. Now, as I glance around, I notice younger women stepping confidently into the spaces I used to occupy. It's both humbling and exhilarating to see the tides of influence shift.

Society, of course, now loves to glorify youth. Young entrepreneurs are smashing barriers, dominating industries, and disrupting the status quo in nothing short of awe-inspiring ways. Governors, senators, millionaires—many haven't even turned forty. The landscape has transformed, and I'm here for it.

But let's remember that with this shift comes fresh challenges. Ageism has evolved as companies prioritize hiring younger talent for their innovative ideas (and, let's be honest, their lower salaries). It's not just about valuing youth—it's about undervaluing experience. And when you layer ageism with sexism, racism, and classism, you end up with a perfect storm of inequality that affects us all.

Lessons from the Journey

Despite these challenges, aging has taught me a few things. Here are the lessons I'd share with my younger self (and maybe with you, too):

Own Your Youth

You don't need to pretend to be older to be taken seriously. Your youth is your superpower—it's a source of energy, fresh ideas, and fearless ambition. Embrace it, flaunt it, and let it speak for itself.

Tell Your Story

Stop trying to fit into someone else's narrative. Your journey, with all its quirks and missteps, is uniquely yours. Don't downplay it. Own it. From tongue rings to first promotions, these moments make you who you are.

Value the Torch Passing

Watching younger professionals take the lead isn't a threat—it's a testament to the foundation you helped build. Celebrate their victories and know that your contributions paved the way.

Challenge the Status Quo

Ageism, sexism, racism—whatever the barrier, face it head-on. Each hurdle is an opportunity to advocate for yourself and others. You're not just navigating the system—you're reshaping it.

Be Authentically You

Trends will come and go, but authenticity is timeless. Don't let society's shifting priorities make you question your worth. You've earned your place. Stand tall, stay true, and remember: Your value isn't tied to your age but to your essence.

Yes, youth is exhilarating, but so is the clarity that comes with age. There's something powerful about showing up as your most authentic self, free from the need to conform or prove your worth. Ageism may try to write your story for you, but the pen is in your hand.

So, here's my advice: Embrace the lines on your face that come from years of laughter and frowns, the wisdom, and the strength you've gained along the way. Celebrate every phase of your journey because each one is a masterpiece in its own right.

And when the world tries to put you in a box, smile, shake your head, and say, "Not today."

Chapter 9:
Your Seat at the Table

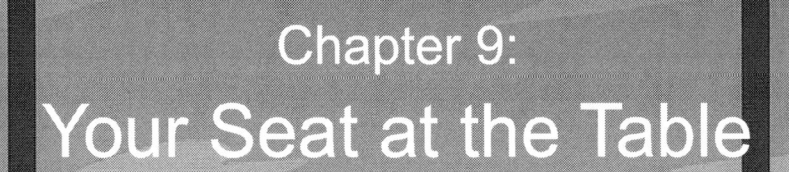

Earning a seat at the table is just the beginning; owning your space and using your voice is equally crucial. In this final chapter, we share how we've broken barriers, claimed our leadership roles, and advocated for others. Together, we uncover the keys to creating inclusive spaces and empowering the next generation of women leaders.

Helene

The conference table is where all the important people sit. All their staff or people below the "line" sit in the row of seats surrounding the table—the seats against the wall. I have seen the table in every large business I worked at and for the nonprofits I support. I don't miss that table.

Depending on where you work, "the table" may be very different. I've worked for many companies. Some had long tables with comfortable seats around them and then folding ones behind them. I have seen that mostly at large businesses. The hierarchy is palpable, with most seniors usually sitting in the middle of the table, facing the door or the wall, with a window (glass office). This strategic positioning grants them a position of power, ensuring they see everyone who enters. Their deputy or next in line has a seat to their right or left, and the rest of the senior people grab whatever chair is open at the table. The back seats are filled in with the lower ranks. If you are speaking or presenting, you move up to the table when you talk and then slide to the back row when you are done. Lastly, the senior people know which seats the power brokers use, and if someone tries to sit there, they are quickly told to pick another chair. To me, this always reminded me of the game of musical chairs. Seats are lined up, and the participants walk around the seats to music. When the music stops, everyone grabs a chair. There is always one less chair than there are participants. The loser usually sits atop another's lap or on the floor as they miss a chair. Early in my career, I was always a back-row sitter. I used to picture the executives playing that game and wished the music would stop.

In smaller companies, the tables were long enough, with enough chairs for everyone to sit. However, having a seat at the table did not guarantee you a voice at the table. This was an unspoken rule, a frustrating reality.

I've had the opportunity to participate in a few nonprofit organizations. I see the same behavior, unfortunately. I hear the words *executive board* way too often. There were pre-meetings with the executive board, then they trickled down what they wanted to share at the open board meeting. Then, those non-executive board members could sit in rows of seats but had to be quiet. This is just as bad, if not worse, than the corporate power tables. And I also noticed that the executive board loves to use their titles a lot—"Director So and So, what say you?"

This is a changing phenomenon in the corporate world. Times are changing, and many companies are becoming more diverse and recognizing the need to give everyone a voice or "seat" at the table. I recently had the experience of working with companies with these values. I can't tell you how empowering that felt. Everyone sat at whatever seat was open. On the nonprofit side, I see virtually no improvement. It's worse than the corporate world. After all, the board is usually composed of volunteers. Those with executive titles believe they deserve the power, the titles, and the ability to make decisions without considering the members' thoughts and feelings. That leads to frustrations and disappointments. It also leads to members distrusting their leaders and giving up on the nonprofit.

Now for recommendations: First and foremost, if you are ever part of the senior leadership team, stop the madness. Sit at an open seat and invite everyone to the table or get rid of the table. And please, do not keep repeating your title. We are all the same outside of that room and building. It has the opposite effect. People do not respect you because of your title. They respect you when you respect them.

My next piece of advice is about empowering others. It is everyone's responsibility to mentor others. You got to the position you are in because of others. You most likely have been taught, mentored, coached, or sometimes coddled by others. When you leave an organization, they will carry on with those who supported you in the past. It would be best if you always had a succession plan in place. Suppose an organization can only survive with you in your current position. In that case, they will only succeed when you are present, and you will never be considered for other opportunities within the organization. We should always empower others and surround ourselves with people who know more than we do. Remember, it's lonely at the top, especially if you believe no one can do your job but you.

My final recommendation is to learn how you feel if you are being pushed to the back seats. See how frustrating it is not to have a voice. When you finally get that seat, vow never to do it to anyone else. The only way we will change this is for the future leaders to do away with it. I'm so glad that several companies I worked with in the last decade of my career understood this. Therefore, I am optimistic that this behavior is changing in the corporate setting. However, in the nonprofit setting, it's alive and well. I'm happy to support an organization but will only volunteer for a title position if I see the table behavior end. I will continue to advocate for ending this behavior. Still, I have yet to have the opportunity to affect the trend so far. Someone may ask me why I won't volunteer for a leadership role. I will be happy to tell them and maybe have an impact. If not, I will sit behind them, play the musical chair song in my head, and hope everyone who needs a seat gets one. And if they do fall, their title will not help them not have a sore ego and butt.

Linda

I remember I was invited to an offsite planning retreat for a small business I admired. It was a long drive from my Washington, D.C. suburb to the beautiful hills of western Maryland. I came into the room (on time, by the way) and boldly sat myself in the front. I greeted the familiar faces warmly and rolled my eyes sassily at those who looked at me like I didn't belong there. I was used to that feeling—What are *you* doing here? I will tell you how I responded. But first, there's another story.

I was introduced to a scientist while at NASA Goddard Space Flight Center. He asked incredulously, "*You* are the CIO?" After a not-so-brief stare-down, I was about five seconds from jumping in his face with a "Yeah, what's up (in Howard University style)?" But he calmed down.

In another instance, my husband and I were at the airport waiting to board our first-class seats. Someone said, "Excuse me, but do you belong here?" I didn't hear the question, but my husband did. He looked at me with clenched teeth, telling me not to move or budge an inch. I looked at the woman defiantly and did not move at all.

Having a "seat at the table" generally means having an active role or influence within a group or activity where decisions are made. Moreover, you are considered necessary and a valued contributor. Your perspective is considered in organizational matters.

Early in my career, I noticed that essential decisions were made in the men's room. I felt excluded but not defeated. One or two of my peers were with our boss in the men's room. They were having a long conversation. I waited for them to come out and asked them two questions: (1) Did you make any decisions in there because I have something to say? (2) Did you wash your hands?

Here are three things to think about in getting your seat at the table:

Carry yourself assertively. Assertiveness is crucial when demanding a seat at the table. Communicate your ideas, thoughts, and opinions with clarity and confidence. Use direct language, maintain eye contact, and speak up when necessary. Be prepared to support your statements with evidence and examples to strengthen your case. Stand your ground and recognize your value.

Build relationships. Cultivate relationships with colleagues who will advocate for you and help you get a seat at the table. To extend your range of influence, make sure you include industry leaders outside of your organization.

Demonstrate your value. Consistently deliver high-quality work, exceed expectations, and showcase your accomplishments (because that's what we do). Highlight your contributions in team meetings, presentations, or performance reviews to demonstrate why you should be included and recognized. Practice praising yourself.

Back to that meeting in western Maryland. I did all of the above and more. I was assertive and rubbed elbows with those I had positive relationships with. Just before the meeting started, the CEO and the Vice President called me out in the hall. A mistake had been made (I do adore the passive voice). The planner should have invited Linda G. to the meeting, not Linda C. I was not supposed to attend their meeting—they invited the wrong Linda.

I was mortified. I was unsuccessful in turning myself invisible, but Lord knows I tried. Reflecting on what could have been an embarrassing moment, I realized I had changed my expectations. I didn't just demand a seat at the table; I expected it. I am *always* the right Linda!

Jackie

I grew up with a big Italian family, and holidays were chaotic. People were everywhere, so you grabbed whatever seat you could at whatever table. When my generation was young, we had a kids' table, mainly because that was the only way to fit everyone comfortably into my grandparents' cozy home as our large family expanded. Once holidays were moved to my parent's house, the kids' table remained for a bit of time, until one day, it was eliminated. It wasn't because there were no more kids in the family; it was because the family extended the table so everyone could fit at it. Don't get me wrong, the kids' table was fun. No one was watching whether we had our elbows on the table or put napkins on our laps—it was the Wild West, and we loved it. So when the fateful holiday came when we were integrated in with the adults, we were excited to be with everyone else, but we also knew some ground rules came with having a seat at the table.

There are many parallels between the holiday tables of my upbringing and the tables at work where folks gather to meet. When starting my career, I was cautioned to know my place in the organization and sit against the wall on the room's perimeter so that the most senior folks—those who mattered to the conversation—could sit at the table. The wall was the proverbial kids' table. I understood that was where I was to sit until I was "grown up," so entering a room became standard practice, looking around to assess seating options and finding a corner to observe like a fly on the wall.

Sometimes, I felt less than others and as if my seating position displayed my capabilities. It was demoralizing at times. While I celebrated that sitting on the outside meant I didn't have to speak, wouldn't have to present, and certainly was not going to be offered the opportunity to weigh in, it also meant that I was silenced in a way. It was as if my voice, opinion, and expertise didn't matter. So why was I even there?

Fortunately, one day, that all changed when I was invited to sit at the table. A new leader had started at my organization, and his mantra was that everyone deserves a seat at the table, no matter who you are in the organization. Furthermore, if there weren't enough seats at the table, we made space to fit those seats on the perimeter. Only when it would be extremely uncomfortable to fit all bodies at the table did he have a first-come, first-serve seating policy for those at the table. This new leader was a breath of fresh air and taught me that we all have roles and bring value to the organization, so we deserve our seats. Remember, there is a reason you are in the role and performing your work, and you shouldn't feel less than others or silenced by where you sit in the room, so never forget to take your rightful seat at the table.

Having a seat at the table also means inclusivity. While interning at the White House many years ago in my early twenties, I learned from my direct leader that the president at the time had a practice of sitting back and giving everyone around the table the opportunity to weigh in and provide their opinion or expertise to the matter on hand. The president did not make rash decisions and was mindful to hear from others. After all, the president had appointed these people into positions as trusted advisors for a reason. I learned how the team felt empowered, energized, and even respected by the simple act of their leader, in this case, the president of the United States, listening to their perspectives and considering them before making a decision. The president didn't always agree with each person, nor did everyone around the table agree. The beauty of this practice is that the different opinions and perspectives shared only strengthened the decisions made with the information on hand.

As president of a government/industry association, I led a volunteer organization with many passionate, opinionated board members who disagreed with each other. My preferred method of leading board meetings was to ensure that anyone with an opinion or expertise could share it in a safe place. Some questioned this approach, and several asked why I didn't make a decision and communicate the path forward without listening to everyone. I pointed out that it was about being inclusive and that these board members volunteered to give their time and expertise to the organization; therefore, we should respectfully hear and consider their perspectives and ideas. While not every opinion or idea is reasonable, I always vocalized that I appreciated the idea and concept. My critics asked why I would say something was a good point or idea, especially when there were several terrible ideas that I, as the president, know would never be implemented. The answer is simple: I wanted to create an environment where everyone around the table felt encouraged to bring ideas to bear and felt heard and valued. In my career, how often did I not speak up for fear that my idea would be considered dumb? How many times did I hold back at the time and then realize I missed the opportunity to shape a solution because of this fear? I didn't want anyone at my board meetings feeling that way. I didn't want to stifle creativity or miss the possibility of hearing the next fantastic idea presented because of my leadership approach and style.

So what's my advice? It is centered around a few key points. First, don't ever be afraid to take your seat at the table if available, no matter your role and what you bring to it. I'll caveat this with being aware of the leader in the room and their preferences, which is why I qualified this advice with "if it is available to you." It bothers me that in this day and age, we have to qualify for it and that there are leaders who do not make everyone feel welcome at the table. In my organization, everyone sits at the table. My executive assistant sometimes tries to hide from the table, and even at the "virtual table," she shies away. Still, I always tell her to sit at the table and call on her when we go around the virtual table to ensure she is included and knows she is valued. You are in the meeting for a reason, so do not be afraid to sit and participate actively at the table.

Second, be the leader that includes everyone at the table, no matter their role. Consider how you would feel if excluded or set aside without a voice, opinion, or sense of value in the room. Don't let others feel that way—ever. Being kind and inclusive is free, but it can cost your reputation to be exclusive and unkind. Such a simple act can be powerful to others and your leadership reputation. If a person shouldn't be at the table for the meeting, why are they invited in the first place? By being open-minded and giving everyone a fair chance to voice their opinions and share their perspectives when they sit at the table, you are setting the tone for the organizational culture. Listen intently and without bias to fully inform decisions and consider the team's perspectives. There is a reason they are there! Not everyone will have something important to say in every meeting, but you encourage creativity and build trust by affording the opportunity. While doing this, you must also create an environment where people feel safe sharing and providing input. No one will share if the space isn't secure and they feel threatened or judged, so be encouraging and positively reinforce when people share their ideas and perspectives. Remember, you don't always have to take them or agree with them—sometimes it is more meaningful to a person that they could share their ideas rather than have their ideas implemented.

Tiffany

I've spent my career earning my seat at the table—but let's be clear, earning it wasn't enough. I had to fight to keep it. Because the truth is, in many rooms, seats aren't just given—they're *guarded*. They're reserved for the familiar, the expected, the comfortable. And if you don't fit the mold, if you don't look or sound like the decision-makers around you, they will question why you're there.

I learned early on that *just being in the room* wasn't enough. Presence alone doesn't equate to power. Sitting at the table doesn't mean they'll listen. It doesn't mean they'll respect your expertise. It doesn't mean they'll see you as an equal.

So what do you do? You *own* your seat. You sit with intention. You command the space. You make it impossible for them to ignore you. Having a seat at the table isn't about luck or waiting for someone to make room for you. It's about claiming what you've already earned. It's about knowing—without a shadow of a doubt—that your expertise, your perspective, and your voice are not just valuable. They are *necessary*.

In the beginning, I made the mistake of waiting too long to speak, thinking I needed the perfect moment, the right words. I assumed that if I stayed ready, someone would eventually invite me into the conversation. But that's not how influence works. The first few minutes of any discussion sets the tone—who leads, who follows, and who gets overlooked. If you wait too long, the room decides for you. I had to learn to jump in early. To set the narrative instead of reacting to it. To ask the question no one else had thought of yet. To challenge the assumptions that felt off. To make sure my presence was felt before the conversation moved on without me.

But it wasn't just about speaking—it was about *leading* the conversation. I paid attention to who held real influence and realized that power belonged to those who shaped the discussion. Those who directed where it went. Those who weren't just responding, but steering. I stopped waiting for permission to take on that role. I made my own moments. I guided conversations, shifted perspectives, and offered solutions before problems even surfaced. I refused to be a spectator in rooms where I had every right to be a decision-maker.

Confidence isn't just about what you say—it's about how you show up. I remember the times I shrank in my seat, questioning whether I belonged. And I remember how that hesitation shaped how people responded to me. So, I made a shift. Shoulders back. Chin up. No more shrinking, no more second-guessing. I stopped softening my words. I refused to start sentences with, "I just wanted to add..." or "This might be a dumb question, but..." because my contributions weren't an afterthought—they were integral.

And when it was time to challenge something, I didn't hold back. Leadership isn't about agreeing just to keep the peace. It's about being the person who isn't afraid to push back, to call out a blind spot, to disrupt when the room is missing something critical. I had to learn that challenging the status quo wasn't about being difficult—it was about ensuring the *right* decisions were being made, even when those decisions were uncomfortable.

I also learned another hard truth—no one automatically sees your value unless you make it *visible*. I spent years assuming that my work would speak for itself, that my results alone would earn me recognition. But in many rooms, if you don't advocate for yourself, no one else will. So I started owning my wins. I made my impact undeniable. I connected my work to results, ensured leadership understood my contributions, and refused to let my efforts go unnoticed. *Visibility breeds influence. And influence ensures that when decisions are made, you're not just in the room—you're shaping the outcome.*

But here's the real shift—the goal isn't just to have a seat at the table. It's to *change* the table.

Because what good is it to be the first, the only, or the token voice in the room? What good is it if the system remains the same, shutting out new perspectives, keeping power in the same hands, maintaining the same tired narratives?

Real leadership means *opening the door for others*. It means expanding the table, enriching the conversations, reshaping the culture. It means refusing to let the next generation face the same barriers I had to break.

So take your seat. Take it with confidence. Take it with purpose. Take it like you own the table. Because you do.

And when you get there—don't just sit quietly. **Shake the table. Flip it if you have to.** Make sure that by the time you leave, no one ever questions whether you belonged.

They'll know.

Afterword

That's a wrap.

So, there you have it—our reflections on the challenges we've all faced. As you've seen, there's no single solution to these issues. Instead, we've each navigated our paths, learning and growing along the way. This journey has shaped us in all our roles—as leaders, team members, wives, sisters, moms, grandmothers, and friends. And through it all, we've emerged stronger, wiser, and more resilient.

We stand at different career stages, yet our bond transcends these differences. Tiffany and Jackie, both in the prime of their professional journeys, hold senior executive roles, blazing trails in their forties. With countless productive years ahead, they will continue to apply the hard-earned lessons of the past, meeting the challenges of tomorrow with confidence and grace.

Helene and Linda, on the other hand, are embracing the transition to a new phase of life. Retirement is not yet in their plans; instead, they find themselves in a place of deep self-assurance. They've achieved their professional milestones, and now, they embrace a "take us as we are" attitude, fully owning their experiences and expertise. They've earned the right to live and work on their terms, rejecting outdated expectations, particularly in the workplace. With Linda's doctorate in hand and Helene, who will earn hers by the end of 2026, they prove that it's never too late to achieve new heights. Linda's encouragement sparked Helene's pursuit of this goal, demonstrating the power of women lifting each other up.

Together, the four of us have crafted this book as a gift to the women who will follow in our footsteps. Tiffany and Jackie extend their wisdom to women navigating their twenties to early forties, while Helene and Linda guide those in their forties and beyond. We hope that within these pages, you find our stories and the inspiration and strength to forge your own path. We wrote this book with sisterly love—a love that binds us across generations and experiences. As you progress in your journey, stay true to yourself, reach for the stars, and never doubt that you can have it all. We believe in and stand with you as you write your resilience, success, and fulfillment story.

About the Authors

Helene Johnson, Founder and President of Next Wave Workforce Consulting is an accomplished executive, entrepreneur, and lifelong mentor who is passionate about empowering professionals of all ages. As a technology strategist and business founder, she brings decades of experience navigating complex corporate and nonprofit environments.

Linda Y. Cureton, Ph. D, is the CEO of Muse Technologies, Inc., and the former CIO of NASA. With extensive practical and academic experience in government technology leadership, she brings invaluable insights into innovation and leadership.

Jaclyn S. Rubino is a dynamic federal executive known for transforming government operations through strategic leadership and innovation. With deep expertise in procurement, policy, and program management, she champions equity, excellence, and the advancement of future leaders.

Tiffany Bailey is a visionary C-suite executive with over two decades of leadership in the federal sector. Renowned for building inclusive teams and mentoring emerging leaders, she drives impact through authenticity, innovation, and strategic foresight.

"We are not bossy, just aggressively helpful."

For too long, women in leadership have been judged for their ambition, labeled "bossy," or told to dial back their confidence. This book is a rallying cry for every woman who refuses to be confined by outdated stereotypes and societal expectations.

Drawing on the hard-earned wisdom of four women from different generations, *Journey of Women Leaders* is an unapologetic guide to navigating leadership challenges in the modern world. From overcoming gender bias and ageism to mastering the delicate balance between personal and professional life, this book tackles the issues head-on. It's not just about breaking glass ceilings—it's about rebuilding the whole structure with sisterhood, mentorship, and self-discovery at its foundation.

Through candid stories, practical advice, and moments of vulnerability, these authors—two baby boomers and two millennials—share the lessons they have learned while climbing the leadership ladder. Together, they confront the realities of imposter syndrome, office politics, and the emotional complexities of being a powerful woman.

This book isn't just for women in the workplace. It's for every woman who has ever doubted her worth, second-guessed her ambition, or felt like she didn't belong. Journey of Women Leaders is an empowering, irreverent, and heartfelt call to reclaim your voice, own your strength, and lead with purpose.

Learn more about this book at
http://www.journeyofwomenleaders.com

Made in the USA
Columbia, SC
07 August 2025

4a15a812-a112-4b59-a76b-2e9c5e161307R01